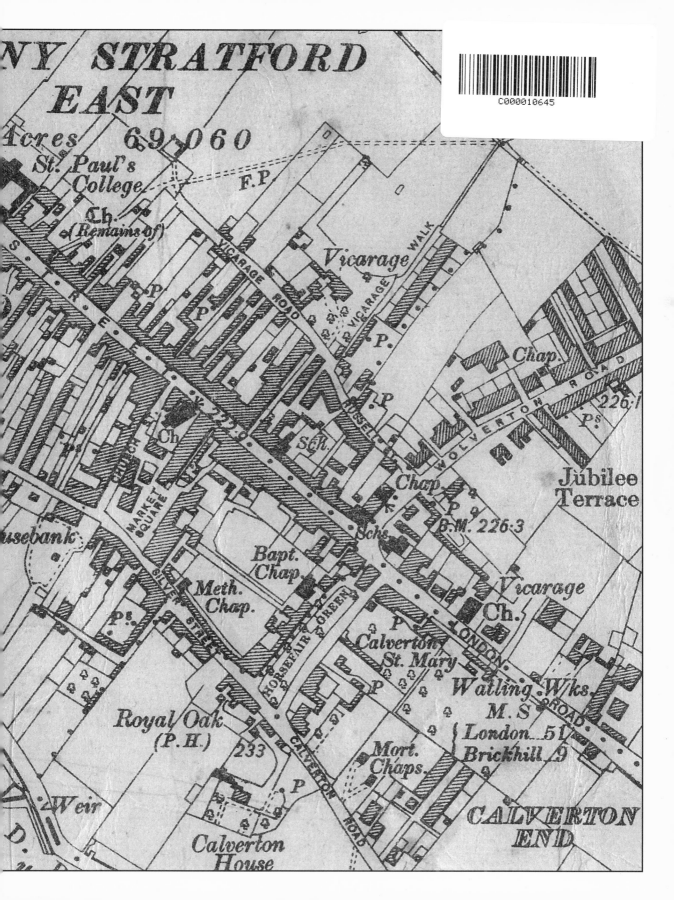

NY STRATFORD
EAST

Acres 69,060

St. Paul's
College
Ch.
(Remains of)

F. P.

Vicarage

WALK

Chap.

WOLVERTON ROAD

226·1

Pˢ

Ch.

Jubilee
Terrace

VICARAGE ROAD

P.

P.

P.

Sch.

Chap.

B.M. 226·3

Schs.

Vicarage
Ch.

MARKET
SQUARE

usebank

Pˢ

Bapt.
Chap.

Meth.
Chap.

SILVER STREET

HORSEFAIR GREEN

P

Calverton
St. Mary

P

LONDON

Watling Wks.
M.S

Royal Oak
(P. H.)

233

CALVERTON ROAD

P

Mort.
Chaps.

London...5½
Brickhill..9

BROAD

CALVERTON
END

Weir

Calverton
House

D.

STONY STRATFORD
PAST

To Sarah, with best wishes

from

Robert Ayers (Bob)
&
Audrey Lambert

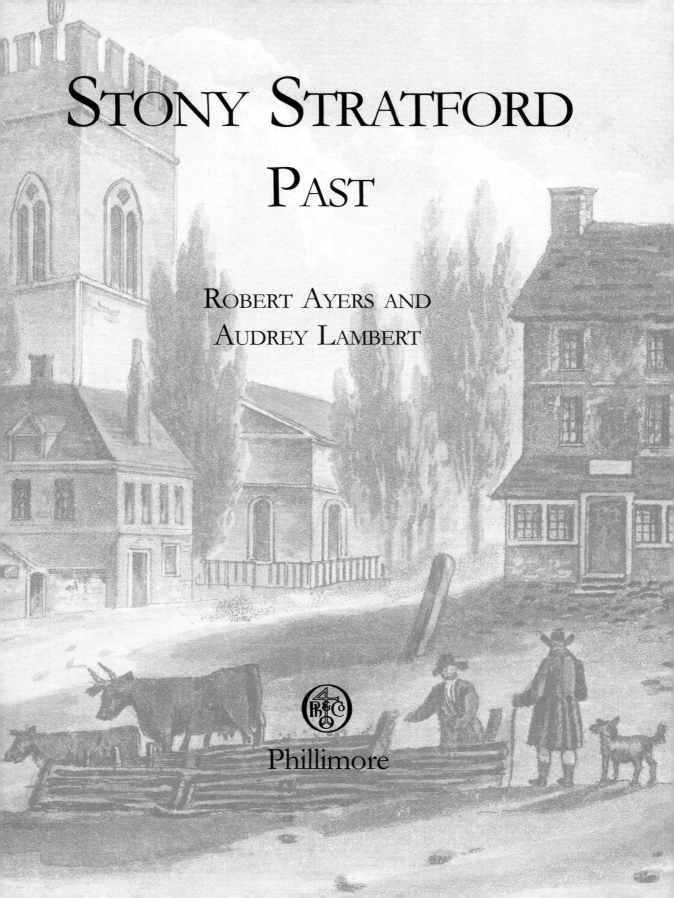

STONY STRATFORD
PAST

ROBERT AYERS AND
AUDREY LAMBERT

Phillimore

2003

Published by
PHILLIMORE & CO. LTD
Shopwyke Manor Barn, Chichester, West Sussex, England

ISBN 1 86077 266 8

Printed and bound in Great Britain by
THE CROMWELL PRESS
Trowbridge, Wiltshire

CONTENTS

LIST OF ILLUSTRATIONS

ACKNOWLEDGEMENTS

This work has evolved over a number of years. Firstly, we must record our recognition of the inspiration offered by two past Presidents of the Wolverton Archaeological and Historical Society, the late Sir Frank and Lady Markham. Secondly, for his patience with our delays in production, our thanks must go to Mr Noel Osborne of Phillimore & Co. Ltd. For information and guidance we are grateful to Brian Barnes, Derick Behrens, Roger Borley and the Ancell Trust, Peter Brazell, Cyril Brown, Canon Cavell-Northam, Mark Curteis, Bryan Egan, Brian Giggins, John Haseldine, John Hill, Eric Instone, Edward Legg, Neil Loudon, John Marchant, Dennis Mynard, Father Ross Northing, Ken Plummer, Michael Ryan, Sue Starr, Ron Unwin, Jean Wellcome, Keith Wilyman, Paul and Charmian Woodfield, Bob Zeepvat and many others. Over some 40 years we have valued our relationship with the County Archivists: at Aylesbury, Jack Davis, Hugh Hanley and Roger Bettridge; at Northampton, Patrick King, Rachel Watson and Sarah Bridges, together with their staff. Photographic assistance has been provided by Ray Rowlson, Roger Welling and Busiprint; technical assistance by Melanie Hickman of Northampton and Peter Cook of Phillimore & Co. Ltd.

ILLUSTRATION ACKNOWLEDGEMENTS

Illustrations are reproduced by kind permission of the following:
Aerofilms 1; Brian Barnes 26, 33, 40; Fred Bavey 29; Les Braggins 148; Peter Brazell 38, 127; Marjorie Bull 115; Ann Burman 3, 80, 88; Canon C. Cavell-Northam 41-3, 49, 90, 95-100, 117-8; Denis Chipperfield 145; Ruth Clare 56; Gladys Cropper 85; Philip Cross 140; Paul Easter 60; Pam Egan 45; Frith Collection 79, 143; Nicholas Fuller 139; Lord Habgood 89; John Haseldine 13, 24, 27, 91, 110; Irene Holland 109; Evelyn Holbrook 2, 21, 32, 45, 101, 121; Reg Holman 125; Malcolm Hooton 20; Marion Hyde 67; Eric Instone 73; Vera Keeling 58; Margaret Ladd 50; Jim Lambert 15; Neil Loudon 103, 105; Les Lovesy 55; Pat MacCulloch 59; Peggy Martin 75; Wendy Maycock 57; Stanley Meadows 113, 128; Milton Keynes Gazette 104, 141; Northamptonshire Record Office, the Phipps Brewery Collection 71-2, 81, 83, 86, 137; Richard Odell 61, 76; John Osborne 34; Doreen Phillpotts 78; Mary Rogers 66; Anne Rowledge 44, 122; Syd Sharp 92-3; Skyviews 126; Betty Sutton 54; Thelma Spires 123; Jean Starsmore 14; Sue Starr 144; Stony Stratford Bowls Club, per John Hill 31; Elizabeth Thomson 63; Daphne Tween 136; Roger Warwick 84, 135; Bill West 9, 36, 74, 146; Keith Wilyman Collection 52, 112, 130, 134; Wolverton & District Archaeological and Historical Society Collection 6, 23, 106, 108, 111, 119, 124; Dot Wood 4; Eileen Wray 68; David Yates 39, 82. Other illustrations are from the authors' collections.

INTRODUCTION

What more can be said about the small town of Stony Stratford and its two parishes, East and West? There are two books still in print: *A History of Stony Stratford* by F.E. Hyde and S.F. Markham and *Stony Stratford: The Town on the Road* by Dr O.F. Brown. Added to these are a number of photographic collections, principally Audrey's three selections in the series, *Around Stony Stratford in Old Photographs* (Sutton, 1994-2000) which illustrate it well. In this work we include many photographs that have not been published elsewhere.

So, what is our aim? Briefly, we do not intend to regurgitate facts that are already in print unless it is essential for continuity, but to update or expand topics where necessary, and to take the opportunity to introduce lesser-known characters in our town's history. In addition to the indigenous population, there were people who came into the town at various periods in history from all over the country. In a brief work of this scope it is not possible always to go into great detail. Some items are the results of our own researches in original documents; others bring together episodes from sources that are less well known; in this process we intend to steer clear of certain 'Cock-and-Bull' stories! However, above all other considerations, the central theme must be Watling Street, the changes that have affected it, and those to whom it has brought work.

Inevitably, with the growth of Milton Keynes and the demand for housing in Stony Stratford, there are now many 'newcomers' in the area again, just as there were after the coming of the railway in the 1840s. As natives of the town ourselves, we hope that we will have passed on sufficient detail to give a flavour of the strands of our history and to enable people, places and activities of the past to be appreciated.

I *Aerial view of Stony Stratford* c.*1968 illustrating how the Watling Street has dominated the town. It shows most of the two ancient parishes of Stony Stratford, East and West, with Wolverton St Mary's top right.*

One

SETTING THE SCENE

'Stony Stratford is a mile in length, including Old Stratford, which is in Northamptonshire, and appears to travellers to be all one town, being divided only by a stone-bridge, across the river Ouse, which separates the counties of Northampton and Bucks.' So begins the entry for the town from the *Universal British Register*, issued at the end of the 18th century. It continues: 'It consists of one uniform street, called the High Street, through which the great Chester road passes. Here is a neat market place on the left coming into the town from London, and behind St Giles's church (the Market Square today). The horse-fair (Horsefair Green) is in a street which fronts the traveller as he descends the hill, coming from London; and the cow-fair (Silver Street) is kept in a back street that leads from the

2   Cock Hotel, c.*1920: this was the principal inn in the town for the 18th-century traveller. Its customers are said to have vied with those of the* Bull *to tell the kind of tall story we now describe as a 'Cock and Bull story'.*

I

3 *The sign, left, is hanging on the* Bull Hotel*; next door the two men are standing outside the grocer's, French and Spencer, also an agency for Gilbey's wines. The* Donkey Shop *is in the foreground right, so-named because its owner, Mr Hall, delivered goods from a donkey-cart.*

4 *Sale of stock by E. Garnett on 7 February 1868.*

horse-fair to the market-place. There are houses on each side of the road as you enter the town from London; those on the right are called Wolverton End, and on the left Calverton End, on account of their belonging to two villages of the same names …' So far, an 18th-century traveller would not get lost in the Stony Stratford of 2003!

However, read on: 'There is no magistrate residing in the town, yet here is a justices meeting held the first Friday in every month, at the *Cock* and *Bull* inns, by turns, by two magistrates in the neighbourhood ... There is no manufacture carried on in this

5 *Pens for the cattle market held on the Market Square, c.1910. Note the elaborate lamp on the* Crown Inn.

town or neighbourhood, the lace-trade among the women excepted; so that the road and market, are its chief support. The market is on Friday, at which there is a great deal of butchers' meat, as the butchers of Towcester and the villages bring large quantities.'

What does the *Universal British Register* tell us on the subject of Stony Stratford as a market town? 'Here are great quantities of corn bought and sold on market days, though very little to be seen exposed to sale in the market-house, as the farmers and corn-factors bring samples to several public-houses, where the chief business of the corn-trade is carried on.'

What about the fairs? 'There are charters for four fairs; but only one of them is of any account, which is old St Mary Magdalen, held

on 2 August, and chiefly consists in cattle and toys. Here is a new statute-fair for hiring servants, held on the Friday before Old Michaelmas-day.'

Nearly 20 years later Holden's *Annual London and County Directory* of 1811 concisely summed up Stony Stratford as 'containing 224 houses and 653 inhabitants, the principal employment of the women consists of Lace-making, but the chief support of the town is from the passage of travellers … Although this town comprises two parishes, it is said that there are not 20 acres of land in both, more than the houses are erected upon'. The population today is said to be about 8000.

The following analysis shows the number of persons recorded against various trades and occupations in Stony Stratford as listed in the *Universal British Register* (1793-8):

Occupations and Trades: 1790s, Stony Stratford

gentry	10	ironmongers	4
clergy	4	labourers	3
surgeons	2	lace pattern-worker	1
attorneys	3	linen and woollen-draper	1
nobility	nil	maltsters	3
bakers	8	masons	3
banker	1	matmakers	2
basket-maker	1	milkman	1
bellman	1	miller	1
boarding school	1	painter	1
(ditto.), for girls	1	parish clerk	1
brazier	1	perfumer	1
breeches-makers	2	plumbers	2
bricklayers	5	potash-maker	1
butchers	3	saddlers and harness-makers	2
cabinet-maker	1	salesman	1
carpenters	9	sawyer	1
carrier	1	schoolmaster	1
clerk of works	1	shoe makers	5
clock and watchmaker	1	shoe warehouseman	1
coach-maker	1	smiths	3
collar-maker	1	smith and farrier	1
coopers	4	stationer	1
currier	1	staymaker	1
drapers	4	surveyor of houses and windows	1
excise-officer	1	tailors	5
farmers	2	tanner	1
fellmonger and wool-dealer	1	tinman	1
fisherman and netmaker	1	toyman	1
fishmonger	1	toy warehouseman	1
gardeners	4	toyseller	1
glaziers	2	upholsterer	1
grocers	15	victuallers	16
haberdasher	1	wheelwrights	2
hairdressers	3	wine and brandy merchant	1
hemp-dresser and roper	1	woollen-draper	1
innkeepers	3		

Two

AT THE CROSSROADS

Stony Stratford grew out of the parent villages of Calverton and Wolverton, straddling the Roman Watling Street at a ford on a bend of the river Ouse. The ford subsequently was replaced by a causeway and bridge in the 13th century. A market was granted on 30 April 1194 by King Richard I to Gilbert Basset and his wife Egelina. The latter had been married previously to one of the powerful de Bolbecs. This grant of a market was confirmed by King John on 12 March 1200. The first dwellings in Stony Stratford are documented at about the same time. Stony Stratford West was to appear first as a separate manor in 1257 whilst the Wolverton side, Stony Stratford East, appeared in the 16th century.

Thus, Stony Stratford was to develop as a New Town of the 12th and 13th centuries out of Calverton and Wolverton parishes. New Wolverton or 'Wolverton Station' was built as the first railway town in 1838 to the east of Stony Stratford, in the remaining part of Wolverton parish. The civil parish of Stony Stratford was absorbed in Wolverton on the formation of the Wolverton Urban District Council in 1919: hence one has to search under 'Wolverton' when researching material at places such as English Heritage in Swindon. History repeated itself in 1967, when these places were included with other towns and villages in this part of north Buckinghamshire, in a master plan for a large

6 *Possibly the earliest deed from Stony Stratford, c.1214-47, this describes a grant by William son of Hamo to Hamo Hasteng of £20 rent in Stratford which Alan son of Hamo, his brother, gave to the said Hasteng. (MS Radcl. dep. deeds 243)*

7   *Map by Owen and Bowen of the road from Stony Stratford to Market Harborough. It comes from* Britannia Depicta or Ogilby Improved, *a road atlas issued between 1720 and 1764.*

new town named after one of the constituent villages, Milton Keynes. Only what remained of rural Calverton was excluded officially from the development, at least for the present!

So how did Stony Stratford evolve? The antiquarian writers of the 18th century, such as Thomas Pennant in *The Journey from Chester to London*, 1782, still assumed that the Roman settlement of Lactodorum was at Stony Stratford: this honour is today conceded to the nearby town of Towcester. The Roman settlement to the south was Magiovinium on Dropshort farm, Fenny Stratford. Villa sites and Roman remains have been found near Stony Stratford at Bancroft, Cosgrove, Furtho, Deanshanger and Thornborough, but there has not been any conclusive evidence of important finds in the town itself, despite rumours over the years to the contrary. Then, of course, there are the fifty to sixty silver and gilt bronze plaques and other objects found in the Windmill Field between Passenham and Old Stratford in 1789 – are these finds evidence of an undiscovered Roman temple?

Consequently, artefacts discovered at Stony Stratford, are considered to have been left by travellers passing through the area on the east-west ridgeway routes, north-south along Watling Street, or even following the various skirmishes in the vicinity. Regrettably the now-defunct, but prestigious, archaeological unit of the Milton Keynes Development Corporation had enough on its hands to cope with the wide-ranging growth of housing in the centre of Milton Keynes, than to look in depth at the older settlements on its borders.

Coming to Saxon times, the Anglo-Saxon Chronicle recounts that in A.D.921 King Edward the Elder, the son of Alfred the Great, was at Passenham, the parish just across the river Ouse in Northamptonshire and adjacent to that part of Calverton, where Stony Stratford East was to develop. The chronicler records that Edward sent the levies of the kingdom of Wessex to Passenham and encamped there, whilst the fortress at Towcester was being reinforced by a stone wall. Jarl Thurferth and his Scandinavian

8 *Market Square and Oxford Street, seen from St Giles church tower* c.*1905, look out towards Passenham across open fields.*

9 *The southern end of Silver Street at the corner of Horsefair Green,* c.*1914. The War Memorial was built at this end of the Green in 1920. On the right is the* Royal Oak *which closed in March 1961.*

10   *Vicarage Road, c.1912, formerly Back Lane; on the right are buildings that indicate the divisions of the medieval burgage*
plots.

barons submitted to Edward as their lord and protector. This reference to the Danelaw demonstrates only too well that this area of Watling Street was often a boundary between opposing forces.

Although Stony Stratford does not feature in Domesday Book of 1086, modern historians nevertheless have argued that the descriptions of Calverton and Wolverton contain a 'hidden element', that can only mean that dwellings were beginning to spring up along *Watlingestret* at that time, but written records first mention plots of land a century or so later. There is also the question as to where such development started. Did it begin on the higher ground at what we now call Old Stratford, or was it at the northern end of Stony Stratford near the bridge?

Certainly there were buildings at the bridge end; for example, in the will of Thomas Posenest of 15 January 1494/5 there is reference to the 'hermitage of St John by Old Stratford'.

One can imagine that the devastating fire of 1742 removed evidence that would have helped us to resolve this question today. For example, Camden stated that 113 houses were destroyed in 1742 in Stony Stratford, whereas press reports of the time quoted a figure of 146 houses in Stony *and* Old Stratford, so possibly there was a cluster of cottages on the Old Stratford bank that was destroyed by the burning, wind-blown thatch. Incidentally, one of those little geographical quirks in parish boundaries was sorted out in 1883 when a detached part of Calverton parish, the Bridge

11 *Interior of the Catholic church of St Mary Magdalene, built in 1959 on the site of St Oswalds, the house that was 105 High Street.*

Meadows on the south-western side by the Ouse Bridge, was at last added to Stony Stratford West.

Medieval Stony Stratford developed on its burgage plots on either side of Watling Street, with its churches, inns, hostelries, markets and merchant families, within a compact framework that still exists today. In the 13th century the name of the town was written in many forms, such as *Stani Stratford, Strafford, Stratfordia, Stony Stretteford*; in 1491 it was recorded as *Stonyng Stretford*. In the 1950s the spelling was still being varied as *Stoney Stratford*.

Professor Hyde judged that as the baronial power of Wolverton declined, so the centre of gravity passed gradually from the hands of the old land-owning families to a newer class

of land magnate, to men who had acquired fortunes in trade and who wished to safeguard their wealth against undue price fluctuations by investing it in land. In turn they re-let their land to tenant farmers, to cattle raisers, and to sheep grazers. 'In Stony Stratford the importance of the older families such as the Hastynges, the de Hyntes, the Anketyls and the manorial overlords, de Veres, de Calvertons and de Wolvertons dwindles before the Smiths, the Taillours, the Brasyers, the Hayles, the Rokys, the Lawes and the Edys. Through the ownership of land and property within the town, they gave to Stony Stratford a unity which it never possessed before.'

On either side of Watling Street, we can still see that there was also a back, 'service'

12   *Passenham water-mill, c.1910. Built in the mid-17th century, it ceased operations about 1920.*

13   *Stony Stratford mill, c.1930. The river Ouse approaches the mill from the left, whilst the mill race is seen on the right.*

road. We can recognise Stony Stratford West bounded by the western side of the High Street, the northern side of Horsefair Green, round to Silver Street, Horn Lane and Mill Lane. The other parish, Stony Stratford East, was bounded by the eastern side of the High Street, the northern side of Wolverton Road from the High Street, but only that short section as far as Russell Street. The latter street was then part of Back Lane which included also the present Vicarage Road and came out into the High Street beyond St Mary Magdalen's churchyard. Nevertheless, these parishes were still very small areas: it was said that the town's size accounted for only 70 acres when compared with the 4,240 acres of its mother parishes.

However, modest expansion of the small original township took place in the 19th century along Wolverton Lane (now Road), and on the Watling Street at London Road, in Wolverton End and in Calverton End; many of these houses were for workers at the new factories in Wolverton. Until 1953 the church of St Mary the Virgin in London Road was known confusingly as Wolverton St Mary. To add to this complexity, the doctor's house opposite the church was called Calverton Limes, but the position was even more complicated when occupied by the building-parson, W. P. Trevelyan; it was listed in *Kelly's Directory* as 'Calverton St Mary's, Wolverton St Mary'. Then it seems to have reverted to Calverton Limes under Colonel Hawkins. Another large house, Calverton Lodge, the home then of a doctor, but now a hotel, was on the northern side of Horsefair Green; Calverton House, built for the vicar of Stony Stratford, with its two lodge-houses, was a

little further along at the south-western corner of the Green. Close to Calverton Lodge, the Cottage Hospital and Dispensary was to be established. Consequently, it goes without saying that care must be taken when consulting the earlier censuses, because the inhabitants can be listed in four different parishes.

The churches were at the centre of the medieval parishes: St Giles was originally a chapel-of-ease for Calverton and St Mary Magdalen for Wolverton. The latter was probably founded in the reign of King Edward I, about the time that his Queen's Cross was erected. The 15th-century towers of both churches stood out as landmarks in this part of the Ouse valley, from the surrounding higher ground. When the body of the church of St Mary Magdalen was destroyed in 1742, its ecclesiastical parish was united with that of St Giles in 1775. The opportunity was taken to rebuild the nave of St Giles to cater for the increased congregation: this was carried out by Hiorne, who also worked on the church at Tetbury in Gloucestershire.

As mentioned earlier, a new church was eventually built in London Road, and a new parish created a little later in 1870. Following another serious fire, this time in the interior of St Giles on Boxing Day 1964, it was decided to review the need for Anglican churches in the town. St Mary's was declared redundant and St Giles church refurbished. In this instance, the two ecclesiastical parishes of St Giles and St Mary the Virgin were united and the parish church that remained was re-dedicated to St Mary and St Giles on 7 April 1968: the first vicar of the united parish was

14 *Aerial view of Warren Farm at Old Wolverton. The cottage, right, was the 18th-century farmhouse of Mr Barrett, having a two-storey front, with three storeys at the back. In the foreground, the new Warren Farmhouse was built in 1899. The site was incorporated in the new town development and now comprises offices except for one barn. The Queen and the Duke of Edinburgh visited it on their tour of North Buckinghamshire in 1966.*

the Rev. C.H.J. Cavell-Northam, who was to serve there for 30 years. One must also not forget in the equation another Mary: St Mary Magdalene, the modern Catholic Church, built on the site of St Oswald's, at 105 High Street some 35 years ago. Appropriately the new church faces the lone tower of the old St Mary Magdalen, which stands on the opposite side of the High Street, by Tower Passage. On a lighter note, one of the many now-vanished gravestones in the churchyard of St Mary Magdalen was said to declare:

> Here lies a body who did no good.
> And if it had lived it never would;
> Where it has gone and how it fares,
> Nobody knows and nobody cares.

Three

ROYAL PROGRESSES

In modern times official visits by royalty have been few and far between. In the 1840s Queen Adelaide, the widow of William IV, and later Queen Victoria and Prince Albert, all progressed from Wolverton railway station through Stony Stratford to the Duke of Buckingham's mansion at Stowe. Edward, Prince of Wales, was often in the neighbourhood before the Second World War; the present Queen and the Duke of Edinburgh were on Stony Stratford's Market Square in April 1966, during an official visit to North Buckinghamshire, just before the building of the new town of Milton Keynes.

However, in the early history of the town the royal court was often in the locality. King John dated Letters Patent from Stony Stratford in 1215 and Henry IV in 1409. Queen Margaret of Scotland wrote to Henry VIII from the town in 1516 and Henry himself sent letters from there on 8 and 20 September 1525. He was there also in 1540, when one of the tapsters, who had vagrantly followed the court and enhanced the price of victuals, was

15 *Queen's Oak, Potterspury, c.1880. The cowman is named Earles.*

16 *This watercolour of 1789 by Thomas Trotter depicts the manor at Grafton Regis, Northamptonshire. The medieval house was the home of Elizabeth Woodville.*

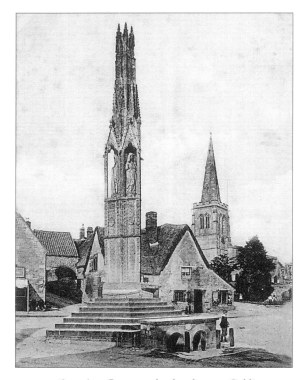

17 *Queen's Cross and church at Geddington, Northamptonshire, c.1907. Following the death of Queen Eleanor of Castile on 28 November 1290 at Harby in Leicestershire, the queen's body was carried to Westminster Abbey. This is one of the 12 memorial crosses commissioned by her husband King Edward I to mark the places where the cortege rested: this Cross is thought to resemble most closely the one erected at Stony Stratford.*

condemned 'to sit in the pillory with a paper on his head'.

Much of this activity was because Stony Stratford was close to the great hunting centres of Whittlewood and Salcey Forests. Edward IV hunted there in 1464. After spending the night of 30 April in the town, he rode early the next morning to the manor house at nearby Grafton Regis, which the Woodville family had held for three centuries. There in secret, on the first morning of May, Edward married Elizabeth Woodville, whom he had met first in Whittlewood Forest under a tree, of course now known as the 'Queen's Oak'. Stony Stratford and Grafton Regis both benefited from the marriage, and the Woodvilles were promoted to positions of state. Anthony Woodville was appointed governor to Edward's eldest son, Edward Prince of Wales, and when King Edward died on 9 April 1483, Anthony escorted the young king, now Edward V, from Ludlow, to join his brother Prince Richard in London.

The royal party halted in the area, Woodville at Northampton and Edward traditionally at the *Rose and Crown* in Stony Stratford (26-8 High Street). Shakespeare recorded this in *Richard II*, Act 2, scene 4, through the words of the Archbishop of York, thus: 'Last night I hear that they lay at Northampton/ At Stony Stratford they will be tonight.' Acting as Regent, the Duke of Gloucester arrested Woodville on a false charge and placed him under guard. Sir Anthony was taken to Yorkshire, and to his death.

Gloucester arrived next morning at Stony Stratford, accusing the new king's loyal

18   *This arch at the village of Wicken is an example of those erected at the entrances to the towns and villages on the route that Queen Victoria and Prince Albert took when they travelled by carriage from Wolverton railway station on their visit to Stowe House, the home of the Duke of Buckingham, in 1845.*

19   *Invitation from Stony Stratford Friendly Societies to a luncheon commemorating the coronation of King Edward VII and Queen Alexandra proposed for 26 June 1902. In the event the king contracted acute appendicitis and the coronation did not take place until August.*

20 *Team of bell ringers from St Giles church tower who rang for King Edward's Coronation Day on 9 August 1902. Standing, left to right, are Herbert Tucker, ?, ?, Cecil Valentine, Bert Edwards or Tompkins and Walter Bonham. Seated are Alan Giles, William (Bill) G. Clark, Alfred Clarke, Edwin Yates and ?.*

supporters of 'compassing to rule the realm and setting variances against the nobility' and arrested them, despite Edward's protests; he was taken to the Tower of London on the pretence of being crowned there, whilst Gloucester took the younger Prince Richard, placing him in the Tower with his brother. After this, Gloucester established himself as King Richard III and, ultimately, the two young boys perished.

Nearly 200 years earlier, the town had played a part in the sombre progress of the body of Queen Eleanor of Castile, the wife of Edward I, who had died at Harby in Nottinghamshire in 1290: at every place where the body rested a Queen's Cross was erected. Two of the crosses still stand nearby, in Northamptonshire: one at Geddington and the other at the next resting-place, Hardingstone to the south of Northampton. The cortège then passed on to Stony Stratford and from there to Woburn and on its way to London. The cross at Stony Stratford was demolished in the Civil War, probably in 1646. The antiquarian, Browne Willis, writing about 1735, said that it had stood at the lower end of the town by the *Horse Shoe Inn.* A member of a prominent

21 *Tibbetts' grocery shop at 51 High Street is being decorated for the coronation on 22 June 1911 of King George V and Queen Mary. Next door is the* White Horse *inn.*

family in the town, William Hartley, then nearly 80 years of age, remembered having seen the base still standing.

In 1897 Mr H.D. Buttrum, a local photographer, produced a plan which had been drawn in 1788, showing that the cross stood opposite the entrance to the field belonging to a Mr F. Skevington and was placed between the line of the footpath and the gate. Speaking in 1920 Edward Swinfen Harris seemed to agree with this location, saying that 'the gas house of old days had been greatly enlarged and improved. The site next to it is supposed to have been occupied

by the Eleanor Cross …'. The old 1788 plan also showed what appeared to be a road at the end of the cottages near the gas works. These cottages, demolished many years ago, were marked on the plan as charity cottages.

However, wherever the Eleanor Cross actually stood, the Street Charity took the initiative in 1946 to mark the 300th anniversary of its destruction by affixing a commemorative plaque on 153 High Street. When this house was demolished in a clearance scheme, the plaque was subsequently re-fixed on an archway at some new properties, 157-9 High Street. On the advent

22 *Front of Calverton Limes in London Road, 1906. The building is now used as a Working Men's Club. Note the attractive herring-bone pattern on the roof tiles. The handsome chimney stacks have been demolished and other unsympathetic alterations have been carried out.*

of Milton Keynes in the 1970s, Queen Eleanor was further commemorated by the naming of the Stony Stratford bypass or 'Loop road' as Queen Eleanor Street.

The town celebrated with great enthusiasm the carriage drive of Queen Victoria and Prince Albert from the railway station at Wolverton to Stowe in January 1845. The carriages, preceded by outriders and escorted by the Yeomanry, passed quickly along the original main road through Old Wolverton, to the enthusiastic cheering of the many people who lined the route. There were two triumphal arches between Wolverton and Stratford and five in Stony Stratford, bearing such inscriptions as 'Hail Victoria' and 'God Bless the Queen'. Many houses were decorated with evergreens and hung with flags; the foot-ways were lined with people, among whom were the Friendly Societies with their badges and flags.

There were similar shows of loyalty at the time of the Queen's Diamond Jubilee in 1897, with banners across the High Street, and the waving of flags. There are a number of photographs taken in 1902, showing the town's procession, celebrating the coronation of King Edward VII as well as in 1911 for George V. Leaping the century, the tradition was maintained in 2002, with a fine show of decorations for Queen Elizabeth II's Golden Jubilee.

Four

AT THE CROSSROADS AGAIN:
THE CIVIL WAR

Stony Stratford was literally at the crossroads at the time of the English civil war. On its eve, the Tyrrells of Thornton and the Bennets of Beachampton were for Parliament, whilst the Longuevilles of Wolverton and Bradwell, with the Cranes of Loughton and the Fortescues of the Shenleys, were for the King.

The situation was ripe for frequent skirmishes in the district.

In the early part of 1643 the Royalists held Stony Stratford and Grafton Regis; the Parliamentary forces were at Newport Pagnell and Aylesbury. In February, it was reported that Captain Sanders and a dozen of his troops

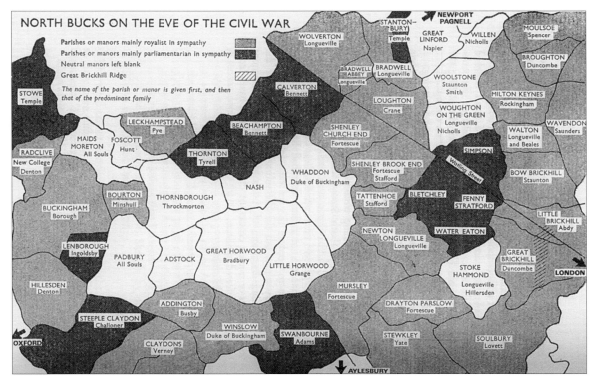

23 *A map of the area at the time of the Civil War, showing the names of the parishes or manors and the prominent families involved, together with an indication of their sympathies with the royalist or parliamentary causes.*

24 *A mounted regiment with horses rest on the southern side of Horsefair Green while taking part in the extensive military manoeuvres of 1913.*

had been quartered at Buckingham and intended to plunder Stony Stratford, because it did not bring in 'their money that it was taxed with'. In December 1643 Grafton Regis fell to Parliament and, on Christmas Day, the old Woodville manor house was razed to the ground, before the force returned to Newport Pagnell.

The progress of the war can be seen through the eyes of Sir Samuel Luke, the governor at Newport. On 22 June 1644, Leonard Sharpe reported to him that a royalist brigade of about five hundred men had quartered at Bicester, the previous night, and was going to be at Stony Stratford that night. On 20 October, Luke wrote to Robert, Earl of Essex that last night a party had come to Stony Stratford to outface them and that, for the want of foot-soldiers, they could not 'so much as send out to look after them'. In December again, writing to Essex, he complained that the Committee of Northampton had failed him in its promises to send in a party and that Captain Andrewes, finding the guards too strong, had retreated to Stony Stratford without doing anything. He added, 'I forbear to send up my prisoners yet, because I hear that there are fifty of the King's horse on the road.' In February 1645, the term 'Roundhead' came into use, with the establishment of the New Model Army.

In the period 9-12 June 1645, Luke's correspondence referred more and more to the town. On 9 June, he wrote to Sir John Norwich 'to acquaint you that Sir Thomas Fairfax ('The General') has ever since Saturday quartered at Sherington and is this day marched to Stony Stratford, his Majesty's army being at Daventry, his Majesty being in person, and Prince Rupert (of the Rhine)

abroad towards Nottingham or Derby with a party …'

Luke learned on 10 June that the King was stationed at Daventry with his ordnance on the hills. 'We think he stays for aid or to force us to fight in disadvantage. Tomorrow the army marches early towards the enemy … I hope the Lord will be with this poor condemned army.' The following day he stated that he was confident that if the young colonels of the Roundhead army should advance over the water, the enemy would retreat. Oliver Cromwell himself linked up with the New Model Army on 13 June; on the next day Charles was defeated decisively by Cromwell and Fairfax at the Battle of Naseby in Northamptonshire. After that, Stony Stratford's part in national history diminished and, almost symbolically, it was to suffer the loss of the Eleanor Cross the following year.

25 *A letter written in 1940 by the secretary for Air Raid Precautions, appealing for volunteers from the Auxiliary Fire Service to assist in blocking fields to hinder enemy landings during the Second World War.*

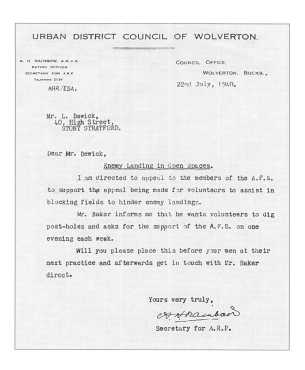

26 *The Home Guard is shown some time after 1943 in the Russell Street school playground in this photo by well-known local photographer Thorneycroft. In the front row are local celebrity athlete, Jimmy Knight (7th from left), one of the town's doctors, E.D. Lawrence (to his left), and William J. Toms, headmaster of the Church School (standing, far right).*

A leading person in the town, Charles Woollard, recalled in a talk to the Literary and Debating Society in 1920, that the Pest House had stood in Horn Lane in Stony Stratford. In the year 1625, between June and December, 113 people had died of the plague. Just before the activity of the civil war, in 1641 the plague broke out again and 102 townsfolk died. Two years after the Battle of Naseby, there was another 'visitation' that claimed 43 lives. So, the population would have been much reduced in the space of a mere 20 years.

Five

THE MALLETTS: A VANISHED ESTATE

Two centuries ago you could walk down Wolverton Lane in Stony Stratford, then down Back Lane to arrive at The Ring, a patch of land behind the *Swan with Two Necks* inn, 92-4 High Street, used for practising and breaking-in horses. Today you go down Russell Street and Vicarage Road, and come to the Ancell Trust sports ground. Before your eyes is the new development of Ostlers Lane, Magdalene Close and Queen Eleanor Street. High on the embankment stands the new A5 road. All of these in the last quarter of a century have transformed the landscape between this part of Stony Stratford and the old village of Wolverton.

Looking at this area today it is difficult to appreciate that the lower part of the sports ground cottage is all that survives above ground of the ancient estate of the Malletts that once adjoined the east end of St Mary Magdalen churchyard and, as Ratcliff explained in his *History of the Newport Hundreds*, extended over several acres towards Wolverton and Old Stratford, and was probably bounded to a considerable extent by the river Ouse. In 1920 Charles Woollard added that 'you may have noticed the fields all around are divided by stone walls instead of the hedges as is usual; these stones are all that remain of the famous building'.

The estate appears to have been first documented in 1487, when it was owned by John Edy, a prosperous merchant, who is thought to have built the tower of St Mary Magdalen church, of which he was the principal benefactor. The property passed through the Pigott, Penn and Rogers families,

27 *Narrow entrance on the right to Coach and Horses lane which led to the former Malletts estate but in later times gave access to St Paul's College, Fegan's Homes, the Ancell Trust sports ground and, when widened, to Fegan's Court.*

28 *Malletts Lane went through what is now the sports ground, continuing as a pathway across the fields and over stiles to Old Wolverton. In the background can be seen the impressive building of Fegan's Homes for Boys before some of the buildings to the left, such as the kitchens, were demolished.*

29 *A parade in Vicarage Road on the occasion of a visit by the Dagenham Girl Pipers, c.1935. Of interest in the background is the stone wall to the old St Giles Vicarage: this possibly utilised stone recovered when the Malletts or the old St Mary Magdalen church-tower was taken down.*

until in 1661 it was sold by Daniel Rogers of Stoke Bruerne to Piercy Longracke of Wolverton, the steward of the de Longuevilles of Wolverton Manor, for the sum of 'ffoure hundred three score and twelve pounds', together with the adjacent Closes. Later the Malletts passed to a local attorney, Edward Jenkins, then to William Hartley and, on the marriage of Hartley's daughter, passed in succession to two other families in London.

The house was described in a sale notice of 1741 as having 'two handsome parlours, a good kitchen and a brew-house, five chambers, a good garden and orchard, the house encompassed around with a moat'. The property was considered suitable for a family or as a boarding- school for young ladies. By September 1758 the situation had deteriorated to the point where 'all the materials of a large old house called the Malletts in Stony Stratford, Bucks' were to be sold. It is said that the remains of the old house were pulled down about 1830, except for a small portion which was retained as a barn until 1865, when

30 *On a first glance this view in 1971 of the gates into the Ancell Trust sports ground seems unaltered. However when Ostlers Lane was constructed through the fields, the gates were re-erected at an angle of 90 degrees to their former position. The cottage, once named Ring Cottage, is all that remains of the old Malletts property.*

Mr Golby thoroughly renovated it, added another storey and converted it into the comfortable cottage that still stands at the entrance to the sports ground. In close proximity were several small ponds, filled in only in the last 30 years, which could well have been the remnants of more pretentious ponds that used to supply the house with fish.

The name Malletts or Mallets was to be found also in Mallets Close – four acres in the late 1600s; and Mallets Lane, later *Coach and Horses* inn yard, and then known as Beckett's Yard after Mr Harry Beckett, who carried out his trade as a coal-merchant from the property, 106 High Street, last century; today, it houses a dentist's practice. The track from Malletts Lane led past what is now Fegan's Court, across the sports ground, Queen Eleanor Street, the main A5 road, and across more fields until it reached the village of Old Wolverton.

Six

Mr Ancell and his Trust

In February 1919 residents of Stony Stratford were surprised to learn that a trust had been established by the will of Mr Frederick Thomas Shillingford Ancell, a retired builder, who had lived at 33 High Street. The trust, which was 'for the benefit of the inhabitants of Stony Stratford', commenced with the sum of £19,467.6s.5d. Before his death Mr Ancell had already sold the property that is now the Conservative Club for £600 and had given

£105 towards the bathing-place, lower down the High Street. The next action was for the executors of the will to give the tenants of the Ancell houses in York Road the opportunity to buy their own properties 'on easy terms of purchase'. Those houses not purchased in this manner were sold by auction. Apparently, the fence at the Mill Lane end of York Road, erected to stop heavy wagons using it, was taken down to make a through road.

A life-long Baptist, Frederick Ancell appears to have been of a retiring nature and had been in failing health for some years. He had inherited property in 1913 on the death of his brother, William James Ancell, who had been a successful architect in London; he had owned property there and in Stony Stratford. Their father was a cabinet-maker and wheelwright.

The original trustees of Ancell's will were Edward Worley, a solicitor, the chairman; local doctor Cecil Powell, together with

31 *Frederick Thomas Shillingford Ancell was a benefactor to the town. After his death in 1919 his will provided for the establishment of a trust for the benefit of the inhabitants of Stony Stratford. The trustees established the sports ground and since that time have given donations to people in need and to deserving town causes.*

Charles Woollard, a member of the long-established Church Street firm of Sharp and Woollard. After Mr Worley's death in 1920, Charles Woollard became chairman of a larger body of trustees, and remained so until his death in 1939. Usually Chairmen of the Trust have been prominent business-people in the town: the present Chairman (2003) is Brian Barnes. However, the one exception to this practice was the election as chairman of local doctor, Arthur Habgood, who served in the town from 1922 until his retirement in 1946, and then lived at Calverton until September 1965. Dr Habgood's son, the Rt Rev. Dr John Habgood, was created a Life Peer after a period in office as Archbishop of York, 1983-95.

Immediately after the Ancell Trust was established, it began to improve the town's sporting facilities and indeed, to its great credit, has been the major provider in the town ever since that time. On what was originally the Malletts site, fields were acquired from Mr Parrott, a solicitor, and from the Wolverton estate of the Radcliffe Trust, together with the field and cottage owned by Mr Calladine. Provision was made initially for five tennis courts, for football and cricket grounds and for a bowling green. The trustees also wished to hold athletics meetings at the ground. Today there are no athletics meetings, but a croquet lawn has been added.

From the inception of the Trust there were donations to many good causes,

32 *The Bathing Place was situated on the River Ouse behind the* Barley Mow *public house, the last building on the left going north out of the town; Mr Ancell also gave money towards its construction. However it is long gone and the pub is now a private house – 185 High Street.*

33   *Brian Barnes, the present chairman of the Ancell Trust, is shown with his bride Audrey outside the Scout Hall in 1953; Ostlers Lane was in the future. Brian's car is PG9715, a Hillman 14; to the left in the shadow is a 2-litre Lagonda; on the right is a Morris Minor 850cc. with split-windscreen HMJ 447; next to that a Vauxhall, ENV125.*

including cases of hardship – people who were ill at home, in hospital or needed to stay in convalescent homes. At that time, sadly tuberculosis was a terminal disease. For the first time in December 1920 it was decided to distribute small Christmas gifts to 180 pensioners and widows of the town: these traditional gifts to elderly townsfolk are maintained today. At that time too the Trust made grants for education, apprenticeships and gifts of tools, as well as funding prizes for Stony Stratford's students at the old Science & Art Institute in Wolverton.

In 1921 the Trust purchased two seats, one to be placed on the brow of the hill at Galley Hill in London Road and the other for Crosshills on the Beachampton road. In the following year it was to buy a second-hand fire escape from St Albans for the Stony Stratford fire brigade. There was a grant in 1933 towards a motor tender for the brigade as well as towards a motor fire engine in 1935.

Back in 1930 the Trust had bought old railway coaches from the Wolverton Carriage Works, for use as pavilions for the tennis and cricket sections. As an aside, when a carriage used by the Croquet Club was recently pensioned off, it was transferred to the Buckinghamshire Railway Centre at Quainton, because it was recognised by the members of the London and North-Western Railway Society to be a rare survivor of the picnic saloons built by the craftsmen at Wolverton Carriage and Wagon Works. The coach has been lovingly restored externally and now only awaits internal work.

To the modern reader it is surprising to note that in June 1935 the Sports Club had requested the removal of 'the German Gun and Motor Van' which were sited at the grounds! It was duly reported the next month that the gun had been sold and removed for a nominal £1, the proceeds being donated to the hospital fête. There was of course no Milton Keynes Hospital in those days, so the Northampton General Hospital received grants from the Trust in respect of patients who lived in Stony Stratford.

34 *Girls from St Mary's School, some dancing round the maypole, at a Hospital Fête in the sports ground, 1935.*

35 *At last the town has a motor fire-engine. Here it stands with its proud crew outside the Fire Station in Silver Street, c.1930.*

36 *Tennis courts at the sports ground, with the lone tower of St Mary Magdalen church in the background.*

How did this gun happen to be placed at the Sports Ground? The story can be traced back to March 1920, when the *Wolverton Express* newspaper reported that the so-called 'Stony Stratford War Trophy', in fact a German field-gun, had arrived in the town that month. Its first temporary home was in an enclosure in the Wolverton Road near the tram terminus, but then it was moved to the site for the war memorial on Horsefair Green. The gun had camouflage paint on it and the words 'Fried Krupp -1918' were on the breech block, but the rifling in the barrel was said to be in bad order. The idea of such a trophy seems strange to us today and obviously the Sports Club was glad to see it go, as it had no relevance to their activities. However, another devastating war was only four years away.

The Ancell Trust was associated with the opening of the Scout Hall in Vicarage Road in May 1937 and with the funding of a club room at that time for old age pensioners. In 1946 it gave a grant to Major S.F. Markham (1897-1975) for the printing of the new history, *A History of Stony Stratford* (1948), which he had written with Mr Francis E. Hyde. This work was the first to treat the history of the town's institutions and its people in any detail, being noted as a model of its time by the great landscape historian, Professor W.G. Hoskins. Incidentally, the trustees were pleasantly surprised when Major Markham in fact repaid the grant.

The Trust's income had been modest since its inception, but its funds were boosted recently by a very generous benefaction from the will of Mr Norman Harris who had lived at New Bradwell in his younger years but, after working abroad, had settled in Maidenhead. Norman Harris had certainly met Major Markham in the 1950s and definitely owned a copy of the history, so we can only assume that this was the tenuous link that resulted in the legacy.

Seven

DEVASTATION BY FIRE!

One can only speculate on the appearance of Stony Stratford before the two great fires of 1736 and 1742. Certainly, little remains today of the pre-Georgian town. That intrepid 17th-century traveller Celia Fiennes and others described Stony Stratford as a stone-built town, but today most historic buildings are of brick, although a closer look at some side and back walls can reveal evidence that they were formerly constructed of stone. There are also walls dotted about the town built with stones that would have come from the ruined nave of St Mary Magdalen church, or from the Malletts house and estate.

Some idea of the scale of these disasters in an area of thatched, closely-packed dwellings can be deduced from the fact that altogether in 1801 there were only 299 houses in Stony Stratford East and West, whereas in the 1736 fire some 55 dwellings and in the 1742 fire a total of 146 houses, including some across the river in Old Stratford, were destroyed.

The 1736 fire started in the Malt-House of the *Plough Inn* on the Market Square and, as a contemporary newspaper report described, 'by the vehemence and fierceness of the flames, which ravaged in so swift and violent a manner that few, out of 55 dwelling houses,

besides offices, barns, out-houses etc. which were entirely destroy'd, had saved so much as their books of accompts or writings.' To meet the damage, estimated at £6000, a collection was organised by the Rev. Leonard Sedgwick, the vicar of St Giles, and William Hartley JP., with the assistance of the two churchwardens and two overseers of the poor. The eventual distribution of the monies for relief was made from the *Swan with Two Necks* inn.

37 *St Mary Magdalen church is shown at the beginning of the article about Stony Stratford in the fourth volume of George Lipscomb's* The History and Antiquities of the County of Buckinghamshire, 1847. *This appears to be a representation of the building before the 1742 fire.*

If that fire were not bad enough, the effect of a greater fire on the east side six years later was even more devastating. It started, so it was said, because of the carelessness of a maid setting fire to a sheet she was ironing and stuffing it up a chimney of the *Bull* on 6 May 1742. Because of the high wind sweeping the flames along the thatched houses in its path, the destruction lasted about four hours, burning down 'nearly all the houses on both sides of the town downwards, and several of those in Old Stratford … separated from Stony Stratford by the bridge and river Ouse, nearly half a mile distant from where the fire commenced'.

The *Bull*, the *Cock*, the *Swan with Two Necks* and the *Three Horseshoes* were gutted, but thankfully were to be rebuilt. However a very great loss was that of the church of St Mary Magdalen, the tower of which stands alone today as a sign of the catastrophe. The antiquarian Browne Willis of Whaddon Hall described how he caused nearly £30 to be expended in setting up, leading and new roofing the burnt-down tower in order to preserve it. The walls were pointed inside and outside and the arches filled up. As mentioned earlier, a consequence of this fire was that St Giles, which had escaped both major fires, had to be rebuilt to cope with the needs of the united ecclesiastical parishes.

Yet scarcely had the appeal for the 1736 fire been completed, than a new appeal swung into action, the trustees of it being the nobility and gentry from a wide area, with the Bishops of Lincoln and Peterborough in the forefront,

38 *Accounts of both the major fires in 1736 and 1742 from issue 209 of* The Cottage Newspaper, *published on 4 March 1859 by William Nixon at 88 High Street.*

39 *William Yates was in business at 40 Church Street as a baker and confectioner, 1883-1915. The board, to the left of the house, advertises that his brother Edwin was a wheelwright at that time and indeed carried on his craft behind the bakery. Note the famous sundial, erected in 1739, possibly to commemorate the major fire of 1736.*

together with such stalwarts of the town as the Rev. Leonard Sedgwick, Matthew Jenkinson and Michael Penn. The centre for the appeal was again *The Swan with Two Necks*, where some £7,300 was collected following the Bishop of Lincoln's 'Brief', (or appeal), and from local contributions. A further £3,100 was covered by fire insurance. Altogether monies received were said to account for about a half of the estimated losses.

There were other large fires. For example, *The Three Horseshoes* or *Horseshoe*, the great wagon inn which was to disappear in the 19th century in the St Paul's College development, had fires in 1703, 1729, as well as 1742. The total damage in 1703 was assessed at just short

of £670; the fire had started at the *Horseshoe*, but spread to the adjoining houses, destroying some '30 bayes of building, besides other property'. The Lord Keeper of the Great Seal, Sir Nathan Wright, obtained authorisation for a charitable collection in aid of the 16 people who suffered serious losses in the fire.

Edward Swann claimed £10 for the loss of pack-sheets, bells, halters and for the loss of work for six weeks owing to burns; Richard Wrench of Knutsford required £21 15s. for the loss of hats and a truss; and Samuel Buckley some £45 for the loss of five horses and of harness for 10 horses. Peircy Eyre's losses were £113 13s. 1½d. for labour and materials to replace the buildings destroyed;

40   *The aftermath of a fire at Fegan's Homes, part of the original St Paul's College, in March 1938. This view shows the quality of the stone and brickwork of the building.*

£30 for hay, £12 for scaffolds, £6 for wood, £4 for a parcel of pit-coals and £10 for 'cyder and ale and household goods'.

William Garnett, a carrier of Levenshulme in Lancashire, claimed £4 for pack-sheets, since it transpired that the John Lee who had carried the goods was his servant. Then a Samuel Brooke of Manchester stated that he had bought in London goods worth £147 4s.9d., which he had taken to Blossom's Inn, for John Lee to deliver to Manchester. Brooke's own wearing apparel and household plate valued at £84 2s.9d. were being carried with the other goods. All were destroyed in this disaster when his carrier John Lee lodged at the *Horseshoe* inn.

Increasingly insurance against fire losses began to be advertised in the *Northampton Mercury* newspaper. We find Abraham Chapman was appointed agent for the Sun fire office of London in 1766. William Malpas – probably from the Market-Place – was the Phoenix agent in 1788 and John Day for the Royal Exchange in 1789. There were still thatched houses in the High Street and on Horsefair Green until a fairly late date. At the end of the 19th century there were thatched cottages near St Mary's church in London Road and a few thatched houses in the High Street in the early 1900s. On Horsefair Green, in the cottage next to the Baptist church, one went down three steps before reaching the level of the little living-room, in which it was said a six-foot man could scarcely stand upright, where it would have been impossible to swing the proverbial cat.

However, over the past 40 years fire-marks have mostly gone from the older properties in the town: these were signs indicating the particular fire offices with which the properties were insured and from which the owners could expect assistance in the event of fire. Examples relating to the County and Royal offices were recorded in the High Street in 1965. Yet still in splendour today above the doorway of 40 Church Street, at the corner of Mill Lane, is a sundial on which can be read the salutary message 'Tempus et ignis omnia perdunt' or 'Time and fire destroy all things.'

Eight

St Mary the Virgin Church, London Road

As mentioned earlier, after just over a century in use as a church, following deliberations as to its future existence, the church of St Mary the Virgin in London Road was converted into a community centre to the design of the architect, David Sim. It is still, however, owned by the diocese of Oxford.

The history of this church and its parish has been well-outlined by Sir Frank Markham in his section of *A History of Stony Stratford* and

41 *The earliest known photograph of Wolverton St Mary's church, 1865. The trustees of the will of Dr John Radcliffe donated land in London Road in October 1863 on which the church and vicarage were built; also a grant of £500 in 1865 towards the endowment and a further £500 in 1866 towards enlarging the church. Another plot was donated in 1867 for the school.*

42   *An early view of the altar and nave of St Mary's church.*

in *The Nineteen Hundreds*, as well as by Dr Brown in *Stony Stratford: The Town on the Road*. Over the century or so of its use as a church a friendly rivalry grew up with St Giles church, which stood in the heart of the town further down Watling Street. As a record of St Mary's it is appropriate to record here its vicars from 1864: they were Rev. H. Hockin 1864-9; Rev. D. McKenzie 1870-2 who later became Bishop of Zululand; Rev. A.W. Mountain 1872-84 whose daughter contributed to Ratcliff's *Newport Hundreds*; and Rev. G.P. Trevelyan 1885-97. The Rev. O.P. Henly 1897-1909 was deprived of his living 'owing to unlawful ritualistic practices'. Then there were Rev. A.J. Moxon 1910-5; Rev. E.

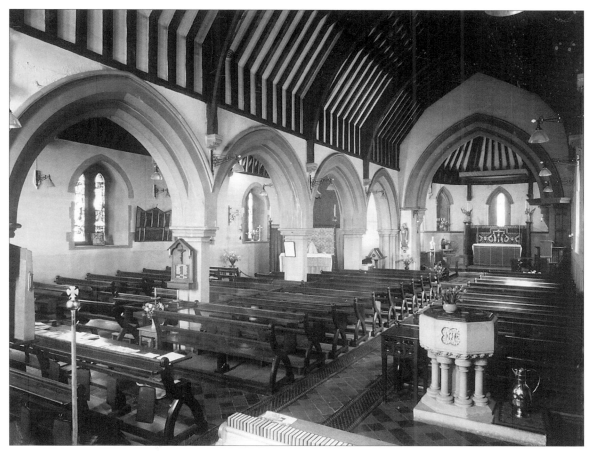

43 *A side aisle of St Mary's in 1950; the altar commemorated the Rev. E.J. Payne who had been vicar there for 23 years, 1926-49. The church was to close after morning service on Palm Sunday 1968.*

44 *The Rev. Edward John Payne, vicar of Wolverton St Mary the Virgin, 1926-October 1949.*

Greaves 1915-21; Rev. C.C.H. James 1921-4, Rev. H.A. Griffith 1924-6; Rev. E.J. Payne 1926-49 (who was a friend of Rev. E.A. Steer at St Giles); Rev. K.W. Wright 1950-7 who went to St Martin's church at Fenny Stratford; and Rev. H.F. Painter, 1957-67.

St Mary's was a close-knit parish with a full range of societies and activities associated

45   *Wolverton St Mary's bible class, c.1912. Noteworthy members are: back row, extreme left Mr Grace. Seated centre, extreme left William Smith, fifth from left Rev. M.R. Graham, then Mr Tingey and Rev. A.J. Moxon, with Harold Phillips on the far right. Second from right in the front row is Mr Bright.*

46   *St Mary's sale and tea on the vicarage lawn in London Road, c.1912; the four earliest houses built in Clarence Road, even nos.104-10, are in the background. The Stony Stratford Town Band is present and in the centre, the Rev. A.J. Moxon.*

47 *An outing of the Girls' Friendly Society from St Mary's, c.1912.*

with them. When they needed a large area for a garden fête or a local Sunday school treat they would use the grounds of Calverton Limes opposite the church or even Calverton House, or they would call on a parishioner for use of his rented field. One Sunday school treat was a visit to Bow Brickhill woods.

In the parish minute books are some out-of-the-ordinary items. In 1926, for example, it was suggested that during the sermon on Sunday evenings and weekday evenings, in all the winter months, the 'gas should be economised' by lowering the light in the body of the church. For the next winter it was agreed that a gas bracket should be fitted over the lectern. In September 1928, it was decided that something must be done to abate the nuisance caused by the noise of

motors passing the church during Divine Service on Sundays. First a letter of protest was despatched to the Chief Constable at Aylesbury and, once he had replied, letters followed chasing the secretaries of the local motoring organisations in an endeavour to resolve the situation.

Wartime brought its problems: in October 1940 there was a small attendance of members because an air-raid warning had sounded just before the meeting. On the same occasion it was reported that 'the possibility of a sale of work was discussed, in view of the new Coupon Rationing scheme for clothes and material, working party to investigate what might be done.' At the next meeting, the decision was taken to provide tea at a lantern lecture only 'if rations permit.'

Nine

MEETING-PLACES OF OTHER FAITHS

For a small town Stony Stratford had a wide variety of religious meeting-places other than the two parish churches. The Baptists had been on Horse Fair Green since the 17th century, at which time they had faced sustained persecution for their faith. They replaced their old church building with the present structure in 1823 and, as will be seen later, the members made a significant impact on the town in the years to come.

Earlier the Methodists had worshipped in a large barn behind the *Talbot* inn, 81-5 High Street. It was their meeting-place until 1844 when the present church was built in 'Cow Lane' (now Silver Street). Their leader John Wesley went on preaching tours all over the country and was at Stony Stratford at least three times in the 1770s, these events being recorded in his journal. On Monday 30 July 1777 he wrote, 'I set out for

48   *General Booth, the founder of the Salvation Army, leads a cavalcade in 1905 past St Oswalds House, 105 High Street, and the Swinfen Harris home at no.107.*

49 *Norman Beechey, a former resident prominent in the town's institutions, is talking to Susan and Michael Fitch who are exercising their ponies on Horsefair Green. Behind them is the Baptist Church, built in 1823.*

Northamptonshire, and preached in the evening at Stony Stratford. Mr Canham had prepared a large and commodious place, but it would not contain the congregation. However, all without, as well as within, except one fine lady, were serious and attentive.'

On the second occasion, on 27 October 1777, he noted that, 'The congregation was large and attentive. So it always is, yet I fear they receive little good, for they need no repentance.' The third visit was on 11 October 1779 when the meeting was recorded only as part of a short tour around the area, including 'Honslip' (Hanslope) and 'Morton, a little mile from Buckingham'. Whittlebury, Towcester and Northampton were also preaching venues over the years. Oral tradition has it that Wesley preached under the elm tree on the Market Square which, attacked by vandals over recent years, shows little resemblance now to the proud tree obviously flourishing in photographs of the Square from the early 1900s.

50   *The Baptist Church was founded* c.1657; *this is a view of the interior in the rebuilt structure before it was modernised in the 1990s.*

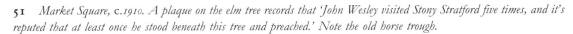

51   *Market Square,* c.1910. *A plaque on the elm tree records that 'John Wesley visited Stony Stratford five times, and it's reputed that at least once he stood beneath this tree and preached.' Note the old horse trough.*

52 *The Congregational Church in Wolverton Road was built in 1823, but is now known as the Evangelical Free Church.*

There was also a Primitive Methodist meeting-place in Wolverton Road at what is today the Red Cross hall, but this closed in the 1930s; its activities do not feature in the local directories. However, still in use as an Evangelical Free Church is the old Congregational building which dates from 1823. This stands in what was once 'Chapel Street', that is, the part of the present Wolverton Road extending from the Wolverton Road junction with the High Street to the corner of Russell Street.

Travelling evangelical preachers visited the chapel of Fegan's Homes for Boys in the High Street: the chief constable of North-ampton, John Williamson, was a popular preacher, immediately recognisable from the distinctive registration number on his official car, VV 1. As to other groups, Salvation Army meetings were held down what was known as 'Bull's Yard', another name for the *Cross Keys* yard off the High Street. General Booth, the Salvation Army leader, was photographed in June 1905 driving through the town on his way to London. Yet another group, the Christian Scientists, had their headquarters at 15 Wolverton Road. The Protestant preacher Josiah Kensit also journeyed through the town in the early 1900s.

Ten

EDUCATION IN STONY STRATFORD

Today there is no secondary education in the town but, if we go back over the last two centuries, we find that there has been a wide variety of educational establishments.

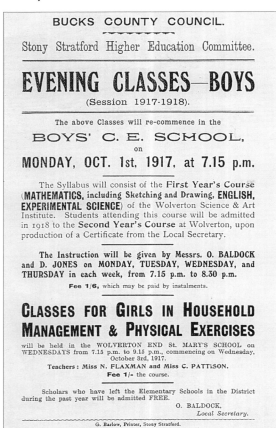

BUCKS COUNTY COUNCIL.

Stony Stratford Higher Education Committee.

EVENING CLASSES—BOYS

(Session 1917-1918).

The above Classes will re-commence in the

BOYS' C. E. SCHOOL,
on

MONDAY, OCT. 1st, 1917, at 7.15 p.m.

The Syllabus will consist of the **First Year's Course** (**MATHEMATICS, including Sketching and Drawing, ENGLISH, EXPERIMENTAL SCIENCE**) of the Wolverton Science & Art Institute. Students attending this course will be admitted in 1918 to the **Second Year's Course** at Wolverton, upon production of a Certificate from the Local Secretary.

The Instruction will be given by Messrs. O. BALDOCK and D. JONES on MONDAY, TUESDAY, WEDNESDAY, and THURSDAY in each week, from 7.15 p.m. to 8.30 p.m.

Fee 1/6, which may be paid by instalments.

CLASSES FOR GIRLS IN HOUSEHOLD MANAGEMENT & PHYSICAL EXERCISES

will be held in the WOLVERTON END St. MARY'S SCHOOL on WEDNESDAYS from 7.15 p.m. to 9.15 p.m., commencing on Wednesday, October 3rd, 1917.
Teachers : Miss N. FLAXMAN and Miss C. PATTISON.
Fee 1/- the course.

Scholars who have left the Elementary Schools in the District during the past year will be admitted FREE.

O. BALDOCK,
Local Secretary.

G. Barlow, Printer, Stony Stratford.

53 *Notice of Evening Classes for boys and girls at the Stony Stratford schools, 1917-8.*

In 1356 there was mention of a *scolhous* which had a chapel of the gild of St Thomas. Later, in 1609 Michael Hipwell left income from his properties so that a Free Grammar School could be established in a barn at the back of the *Rose and Crown* in the High Street. The Church of England tradition was continued in the new buildings erected in 1819 at 30 High Street known as the National School, which had to be rebuilt and enlarged in 1858; then St Mary's School was built just a few years later on the corner of Wolverton Road and London Road.

Those schools were closed in 1937 when the St Mary and St Giles' school opened at King George's Crescent. W. (Billy) Toms, the headmaster since 1920 of the old school in the High Street, moved to be head of this new school. It was a Senior and Secondary Modern school until its closure in June 1968, by which time Mr Jack Read had become head teacher. However, the same premises reopened in 1969 as the St Mary and St Giles junior school, then described as a 'middle school', with Mr John Yates, the former head of the County Primary School in Russell Street, moving there as head. The younger children remained in Russell Street in the Infants school with Mrs Margaret Chapman as head: this is now Russell First School.

54 *A.J. Negus had a motor and motor-cycle business at 25 High Street advertising Pratt's spirit, c.1911; William Payne a fruiterer is at no.27; Singer Sewing Machine Co., no.31 and Frederick Ancell, no.33. On the opposite side can be seen the Church of England Boys' School that had just been reconstructed and the old* White Swan *pub which was to be rebuilt in 1915.*

The Russell Street School reminds us of the nonconformist tradition in Stony Stratford, because the British Foreign and Bible Society School, which had been open since 1844 at the corner of the High Street and Wolverton Road, closed in 1907 and its headmaster David Jones transferred to be head of the newly-built Council School in Russell Street. The work of his successors – R.A. Wright 1924-42, Archie Dormer 1942-60 and John Yates 1960-70 – has been recalled by successive generations of youngsters; as well as the caring nature of Mrs Gladys Cropper who was in charge of the nursery school 1942-75.

However, above all, David Jones was to make a lasting mark on his school and the politics of the neighbourhood. He was born in Worcester, where he won a scholarship to the Grammar school; he came straight from the Borough Road teacher training college to the British school, teaching in Stony Stratford

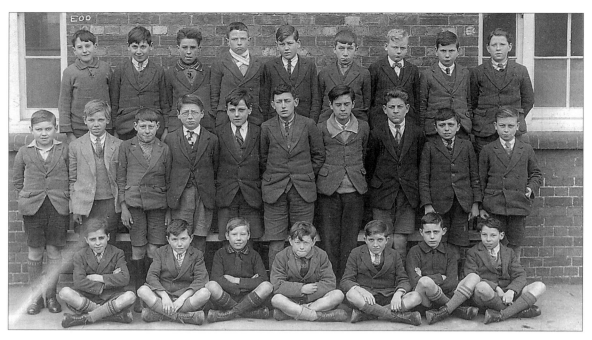

55   *St Giles Church of England Boys School in the High Street. In this 1929 group: back row, left to right, ?, Dick Swain, ?, ?, Charlie Gould, Bert Larner, Lionel Smith, ?, Arthur Webb. Centre row: Doug Higgs, Harry Atkins, ?, ?, ?, Walt Stevens, ?, ?, 'Polly' Underwood. Front row, ?, Archie Caudle, Reg Westley, ?, Percy Pratt, Les Lovesy and Ernie Morris.*

56   *Stony Stratford Senior School group in 1946. Back row, l. to r. Norman Stephenson, Ross Willis, Joan Stewart, Eryl Clark, Margaret Barden, and Ivor Whitton. Centre row: Mr Cheeseman, Robert Illing, Alan Mole, Kathleen Cannings, Betty Shurmer, Ruth Claydon, Kathleen Wrighton, Joyce Colton, Peter Grace, Roy Young and Mr W.J. Toms, headmaster. Front row: May Cross, Mavis Cockerill, Sylvia Benbow, Dawn Rollings, Peggy Hanwell, Pamela Pettifer, Joy Aylott and Margaret Sinfield.*

57 *The British School was built in 1844 at the corner of the High Street and Wolverton Road. Group 2 is seen here with the headmaster David Jones, c.1898. The school was closed in 1907 when the new schools were opened in Russell Street. This building then became known as the Public Hall, being sold in 1998 by the trustees to Mr and Mrs Roger Andrews for use as a Performing Arts school.*

for 36 years. He was well-known for his outspoken views and for the many letters he wrote to the local press. As an ardent pacifist his views during the Boer War provoked some hostility; he was criticised for his idealistic opinions. For many years he conducted a Sunday afternoon class; his addresses every Sunday had large audiences. These classes were recognised for their philanthropic work, in 'bringing much relief to distressed homes'. He spoke also at various large gatherings outside Stony Stratford.

Though he had brushes from time to time with those in authority at the school and in the community, it was said that David Jones gave of his talents to rich and poor alike and he was held in great esteem by both children and parents. An old scholar, R. Ewart Barley, wrote, 'Some months ago I sat with four other Stony Stratford young men, all living in New Zealand … We were all British school boys and each agreed that David Jones had been the greatest influence outside our home circle in the moulding of character and the shaping of life's outlook … From the very earliest days I was attracted by the charm of his language and his exceptional gift of eloquence … Many in the latter years only knew him as the school-master, but in the early years he flamed with

58 *Children of the Russell family at the school in Russell Street, c.1931; at the back are Arthur and Harold, at the front Stan, Vera and Reg.*

59 *The Rev. James Thomas, curate of Passenham and Deanshanger and headmaster of Belvidere Academy, later renamed Trinity College, at Old Stratford, c.1878. He is outside the schoolroom with a group of pupils.*

a holy passion against the evils and iniquities that beset mankind.' David Jones' children were to follow their father as teachers in the neighbourhood.

In the 19th century there were two boarding schools for boys. For some 30 years there was St Paul's College in Stony Stratford, established by the Rev. Sankey who was also its first warden. At Old Stratford was Trinity College, formerly Belvidere Academy, under the Rev. Thomas. Both these schools provided a classical education but both eventually closed; the St Paul's site has been divided into dwellings and offices and the Old Stratford site houses a Saab car dealership.

At various times there were day and boarding schools for young ladies in the High Street and on the Market Square. *Kelly's 1864 Directory* advertised a 'School for young ladies, conducted by Miss Linnell and her sister. They offer the advantage of a sound English education, on strictly moderate terms. The domestic arrangements are those of a private family, and every home comfort is as far as possible provided.' In the 20th century such establishments included the school run by the Misses Stocking in the High Street and York House School, which had been started at Hanslope by the Slade family. The Slades moved to Wolverton Road, next to York House on the corner of York Road (now the Conservative Club), and finally to Clarence House in London Road, to which the name York House was transferred. Today York

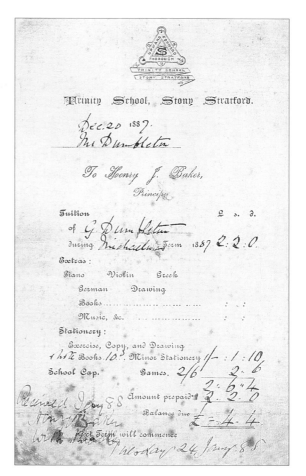

60 *An account of 1887 for tuition fees in respect of G. Dumbleton whose father kept a grocery in Prospect Road. Note the school motto at the top of the bill.*

House houses a youth club. The Misses Slade though ran their school until 1933; it continued under new ownership into the 1950s. Also remembered with affection is the small preparatory school run by Miss Morris at 103 High Street.

Eleven

NEWS THREE HUNDRED YEARS AGO

Although there was no local newspaper in Stony Stratford, by chance the *Northampton Mercury* commenced publication in 1720 and from time to time in its pages we have a glimpse of what was happening in the country town on the Watling Street a dozen or so miles away. Added to this are reports from Aylesbury of proceedings at the courts.

Firstly, referring to outstanding properties in the town, could it be the old 3 and 4 Market Square which were being described as 'a drapers with stable, brew-house, malt-house and a large back-way'? Apparently the proprietor had gone bankrupt in 1723; although his stock had been valued at £700, they would take £400 for it. Diagonally opposite at the north-west corner of the Market Place, a house with a tan-yard is mentioned in 1725 and again in 1760 when Thomas France gave it up. A market house

61   *The* King's Head *inn is first recorded in 1640 but became a private dwelling in the early 1900s; it had an inglenook fireplace in the front room. The inn was originally listed in Pig Market at the northern end of Cow Fair, later Silver Street, but is now 11 Market Square.*

was also mentioned where grain could be securely stored.

As to professions and trades, in 1741 John Farmer, surgeon and apothecary, could be found at a corner house and shop near the Market Place whilst the surgeon John Potter now lived at the newly-built house opposite the *Swan with Two Necks* in the High Street. About the same time there was a bake-house next door to the *Cock* which boasted a 'large oven, a large yard, barn and stable and an acre of grassland.' There was a coffee house in 1728; William Hartley was a draper in 1733 and Henry Potter a glass-bottle seller. We find that James Chinner was a plumber and glazier; Michael Penn a cooper and James Richardson a watch-maker. A brazier named Wilson traded next door to the *Bull*, facing which was a saddler's shop. Thomas Biggs was a farrier; John Roberts a cheesemonger and John Lambert an auctioneer. Attorneys were represented by the 'eminent' George Arrowsmith and by Edward Bloxham, who also had interests outside the town in Fenny Stratford and Towcester.

Francis Mayhew, surgeon and apothecary, took a shop in 1754, not only laying in a quantity of the best drugs but also, since he had attended Dr Smellie's lectures on midwifery, proposing to practise that branch of medicine on very reasonable terms! Thirteen years later another surgeon, named Wilmer, offered inoculations against smallpox.

The clothing trade featured well in the advertisements. John Rock was a tailor; George Mills a peruke-maker; William Bunker a breeches-maker; John Kirby a collar-maker and William Gurden a lace-maker. James Clinton, a son of a lace-buyer was apprenticed to William Dennis, another lace-buyer who set out also to teach him the art of a barber and periwig-maker.

Many specialised items were described when Miss Butler a milliner sold her stock in 1773: a 'variety of plain, striped and sprigged muslins, plain and flowered lawns, silk, gauze &c handkerchiefs, plain and figured 3-quarters', as well as 'irishes, long lawns, dimitties, book-muslins, marcella quilting, Scotch lawn handkerchiefs, men's hose and a number of articles in the drapery and millinery Way.' Opposite the *George* for some 50 years was the shop of a grocer, tallow-chandler, linen-draper and haberdasher. Finally, towards the end of the century Thomas Harrison opened a warehouse and wine-vaults to serve 'fine French brandy and Jamaica rum, British spirits and compounds of every sort, foreign wines of all sorts, hops, tobacco etc.'.

The Inns. The *Cock* was described as a very good accustomed inn and post house in 1721 and the *Swan with Two Necks* as a new-built house in 1730. The *White Horse* was noted in 1738 although the *Universal British Register* was to describe it as 'a neat new building' 60 years later. (The name could have been transferred to a new building, or more probably the original could have been rebuilt.) Another hostelry, the *Barley Mow*, is mentioned in 1739 with fires there and at the *Crown* in 1762. There is a *Black Bull* in 1743, and *The Bull* was described in 1760 as having a large quantity of meadow, pasture and arable land. Long-gone names are the *Drum and Acorn* 1762, *The King's Head* 1768; the *Horse-Shoe* in 1770 in connection with a London to Birmingham stage-wagon and the *Red Lion and Horseshoe* in 1773. Christopher Cook had

62 *Job Jones & Son was a boot-maker, occupying part of* The White Horse, *1890-1903. This wagon inn was rebuilt c.1790; the name goes back at least to 1540. Buildings in the yard, once occupied by a wheelwright and stone-mason, have been converted into private dwellings.*

63 *The main property, later nos.3-4 Market Square, was stone, re-fronted in brick, c.1810; it had been the premises of William Boyes, a draper and influential townsman, for 60 years. Its size can be imagined from the sale particulars which quote 11 bedrooms in the first house and eight in the second. Samuel Holland of Vicarage Road bought these properties in 1896, the year of the photograph. The Health Centre stands there now.*

a stage-wagon service from London to Stony Stratford, Towcester and Southam every Monday and Thursday.

Over the river in Old Stratford a wheelwright's house and shop was advertised in 1728; the *Horse and Trumpet* appeared in 1740 with stables, orchard, a large court-yard, brew-house and wash-house and the more familiar *Falcon* inn had been rebuilt in 1749.

Entertainment. This occasionally made the news; an unspecified, splendid entertainment was given in 1727 by Mr Perry of Old Stratford on the proclamation of George II. Horse-racing is little-mentioned, although a race was reported in 1739 between a roan named *Sappho* belonging to a soldier and a bay gelding that stood at the *Bull*, 'whip him in for twenty guineas a side'. Thirty years later

64 *The* Swan *and* Falcon *inns at the former cross-roads on the Watling Street at Old Stratford; to the left was Deanshanger Road, to the right Cosgrove Road. The horse and trap are about to go over the canal bridge of the Buckingham to Cosgrove arm of the Grand Junction (Union) Canal. The* Swan *is still in business, but the* Falcon *was demolished before the First World War.*

in 1769-70 it was noted that races were held at Wakefield Lawn, the home of the Duke of Grafton.

The sportsman of the 18th century would expect to go to cock-fights. In a notice of a match between some gentlemen of Northamptonshire and some of Buckinghamshire at the *Bull* for a prize of two guineas a battle, it was said that there would be 'very good sport'. Two years later it was the turn of the gentlemen of Hertfordshire and Bedfordshire versus Northamptonshire at the *Cock*, where there would be 'a good chose pit'. Later there was a fight between the gentlemen of Warwickshire and Bedfordshire at the *Three Swans* for four guineas a battle and £40 'the odd battle'.

The statute fair for the hiring of servants and for the show of cattle took place in 1765 when a silver cup valued at £5 was given to be played for a singlestick on a stage in the Market-Place: a singlestick was a basket-hilted stick of about a sword's length used for one-handed fencing. Two years later there was wrestling for a prize of a pair of silver buckles.

The celebrated antiquarian, the Rev. William Cole, often visited the town. His diary shows that in October 1766 he went to dinner at the *Bull* in two successive weeks. The first was to a meeting of the surveyors of the turnpike road. Cole, who was the surveyor for Bletchley, made a complaint against Robert Stevens, the surveyor of adjacent Fenny Stratford, for not laying one load of gravel all the year. The following week Cole went to a dinner on a turtle of about 80 pounds, at an 'Ordinary' or public meal for the neighbouring gentry. This was given by a Mr Bigging of Cosgrove to Dr Forester who in turn had given it on to the public; Cole explained that in this manner Forester had avoided the expense of a large company at his own house. The turtle was 'very well-dressed' with an elegant dinner by Mr Knightley's cook from Fawsley Hall. Then, 'Cards after dinner. The company about 50.' On another occasion Cole referred to a Mr Williamson and his daughter 'from the school at Stony Stratford'.

Entertainment was also brought to the town by travelling players. In 1806 John Malpas considered that there had not been a more respectable company in Stony Stratford than that from the Theatre Royal Richmond. Another group which came there was the Jackman Players; indeed Sophia Jackman was born at Stony Stratford in *c.*1815; the players made another visit in 1845. In addition there was a visit from a touring 'rock band' in 1848: these were musicians who played on instruments made of rock, the idea being to hit lumps of mineral rock with wooden mallets to produce a melody, not to break them! In later years they returned as a Rock and Steel Band.

Education. There was another mention in 1746 of a school for young ladies, in a house and shop near the *Bull Tavern* and corner of the Market Place, being occupied by a boarding- school mistress and a dancing master. There young ladies would be well-

65 *First recorded as the* Angel *in 1677, the name* Barley Mow *appeared in the Constable's Book in 1770; it is now a private house 185 — High Street.*

66 *Mursley Beagles photographed in April 1909 on the last meet of the season, at Stony Stratford Mill. In the centre is Lord Molden, the master.*

educated and taught all manner of needlework. Their ages ranged from four to 16 years and fees were charged at £12 per annum. Later French was included in the curriculum together with 'a particular regard … to the morals as well as the genius of each young lady'. Originally this school had provision for 20 scholars but it was to be enlarged for dancing and dining with room for fifty.

Health. In the 1750s a 'contagious distemper' was said to have raged among horned cattle at Old Stratford and Cosgrove. Additionally, in 1764 a public notice certified that Stony Stratford had been clear of smallpox for some six weeks.

Crime. In the Midsummer Session of 1701 two labourers from the town, Edward Hobbs and Edward Briggs, were sentenced to be whipped for stealing some flaxen cloth from William Gurney of Passenham but Elizabeth, the wife of the blacksmith Richard Brookes, was found not guilty of receiving it.

The neighbouring locality was an ideal ground for highwaymen and footpads. In March 1744 Henry Footman, the chief of a gang of highwaymen in Whittlebury Forest, who had escaped from Aylesbury Gaol, was apprehended at Stony Stratford by a party of General Wade's Regiment of Horse.

Poachers were a problem in Calverton and Beachampton on the earl of Salisbury's estate. 'An honest poor farmer' of Calverton named Daniel Hix had come there to sell some wheat to raise money towards his rent. As he was returning home in the evening he was attacked by two footpads who started out of a ditch. One struck him violently on the head whilst the other rifled his pockets and stole £4 17s.0d. Then there was the instance of a gardener from the town who was robbed and murdered at Paulerspury. A grim ceremony of those times followed an inquest in 1740 on the body of an unknown man, who had cut his own throat from ear to ear. The jury returned a verdict of suicide and he was buried that afternoon 'naked in a cross highway', with the customary 'stake drove through his body'.

Twelve

The Coaching, Canal and Railway Eras

The early state of the roads is emphasised in an extract from the first part of the play, *Sir John Oldcastle*, dated 1600, which was once attributed to William Shakespeare, but is no longer included in a collection of his plays. An ostler says, 'Tom's gone from hence: he's now at the *Three Horse Loades* (or *Shoes?*) at Stoney Stratford. How does old Dick Dun?' To this the carrier replies, 'Uds heart, old Dun has bin moyr'd [mired] in a slough in Brickhill Lane. A plague found it! Yonder's such abominable weather as was never seen.'

With the introduction of the turnpike trusts, conditions on the roads gradually improved. The first local Act established a turnpike from Fornhill near Hockliffe to Stony Stratford in 1706. Others were Old Stratford to Dunchurch 1706-7; Stoke Goldington to Northampton 1709; Kettering to Newport Pagnell via Wellingborough 1753-4; Hardingstone to Old Stratford 1767-8; Stony Stratford to Woodstock via Old Stratford and Bicester 1767-8 and Buckingham to Newport Pagnell via Old Stratford and Stony Stratford 1814-5.

The growth in trade by road was highlighted by the fact that the river bridge over the Ouse between Stony Stratford and Old Stratford broke under the strain of a heavy train of wagons from London to Birmingham, carrying machinery for making plate glass. The last wagon fell between the beams of the bridge. Some 40 horses were needed to drag the wagon up the hill to Old Stratford.

When Charles Woollard gave a talk to the Literary and Debating Society in 1920 he recalled that the large inns, the *Cock* and *Bull*, still remained with good accommodation at the rear for coaches and horses. At one time 60 or 70 coaches and vans passed daily through the town, carrying mails, passengers and merchandise. *The Swan with Two Necks* had been as large as the *Cock* and had rivalled it in importance, as it contained a very large dining hall; however, it closed in 1780. 'The many signs that marked the public-houses were once those of busy hotels and coaching houses.'

Other inns had been converted into private houses. The *Dog and Monkey* stood near St Mary's School in London Road, and the *Crooked Billet* was at the back of the old police station on the Market Square; then there was the *Wagon and Horses* near the Retreat almshouses. Each house had had its regular trade, served by the traffic that constantly passed to and fro along the main thoroughfare. 'It was no uncommon sight',

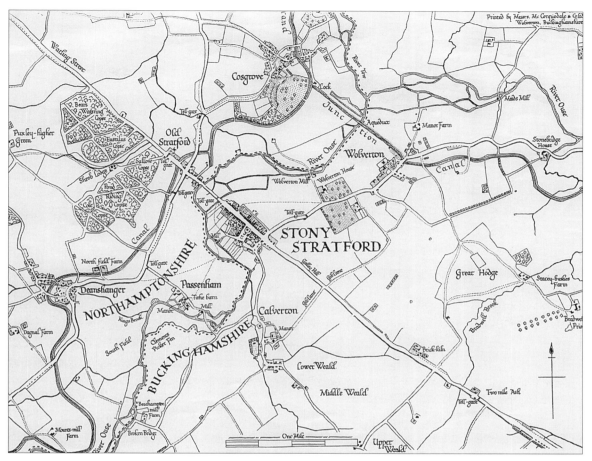

67 *The road network and the canal are shown in this pre-1837 map which Marion Hyde drew to illustrate Hyde and Markham's* A History of Stony Stratford. *At that time there were only a few copses remaining of the great forest to the north of Stony Stratford. The ancient watermills and yet more recent toll-gates of the turnpike age are also shown.*

Woollard stated, 'to see van-loads of prisoners, men and women, chained together in open vans, pull up at the *Bull Hotel* on the way to the coast and thence for transportation to Van Diemen's Land.'

Stony Stratford was on the Holyhead Road and its engineer, the renowned Thomas Telford, believed that the future of mechanical land transport lay with the steam carriage. He was so enthusiastic an advocate of steam road transport that he supported a scheme for the introduction of steam carriages on the road. Although in ill-health, Telford journeyed from London to Birmingham in Sir Charles Dance's steam carriage in October 1831. Boiler trouble at Stony Stratford put an end to the attempt but Telford and the friends who accompanied him were favourably impressed. Nevertheless, shortly afterwards the Government instituted punitive tolls, empowering turnpike trusts to kill off road steamers.

68   *There is no motor traffic in this peaceful scene that shows the climb up to Old Stratford. Under an 1804 Act the Turnpike Trustees were relieved of their responsibility for the bridge over the Ouse in return for a payment of £900. The government rebuilt the bridge in 1835, assumed responsibility for its maintenance and introduced an unpopular system of tolls.*

69   *The scene in the inn-yards of small country towns is typified in this sketch of the* Bull *Yard made in 1908 by Frederick L. Griggs for Clement Shorter's* Highways & Byways in Buckinghamshire *(1910). After the coaching days, out-buildings in such yards were used to house the poorer people of the town.*

Towards the end of the stage-coach era in 1836 there were still a number of long-distance stage-coaches serving the town, all with seats for four passengers inside and either eight or 11 outside. William Chaplin, Benjamin Horne and Edward Sherman were the major operators; others were J. Everett, W. Smith, J. Clare and Sarah Mountain.

London to Birmingham by the *Independent Tally-Ho, Tally-Ho, The Economist* and *Greyhound* took 11-12 hours departing at 7 and 7.45 a.m.,

70 The Prince of Wales *(no.68) and* The Duke of Edinburgh *(no.61), now the* Duke of Wellington, *shown here c.1905, were built to serve the expansion of Stony Stratford along Wolverton Road. Note the tram-lines going down the centre of the road in the town.*

5.30 and 6.30 p.m.; London to Shrewsbury by *The Stage, The Nimrod* or the *Wonder* took 16 hours, leaving at 6 and 7 a.m. London to Manchester by the *Beehive* or *Red Rover* was longer, at 20 hours, departing at 8 and 8.30 a.m. The London to Liverpool service by the *Express* or *The Albion* was timed at 24-26 hours, leaving between 5 and 6.30 p.m.

Return services from Birmingham left at 8 and 9 a.m. and at 5.30 p.m.; times from Shrewsbury were 4.45, 5.30 and 5.45 a.m.; from Manchester at 8 a.m., and from Liverpool at 5.30 p.m. Coaches from London to Halifax, Leeds, Leicester, Northampton, Nottingham and Wellingborough were routed off Watling Street via Woburn and Newport Pagnell.

In 1836 there were two Royal Mail coaches from London by William Chaplin via Stony Stratford. One left London at 7.30 p.m. reaching Stony Stratford at 1.26 a.m. the next day, finally arriving at Holyhead at 10.55 p.m. The return mail left Holyhead at 4.15 a.m., reached Stony Stratford at 1.34 a.m. on the next day and London at 7.15 a.m. The second Royal Mail was from London to Liverpool: it left London at 7.30 p.m., reached Stony Stratford at 1.26 a.m. and Liverpool at 4.50 p.m. The return journey was timed to leave Liverpool at 9.45 a.m. reaching Stony Stratford at 1.09 a.m. the next day and London at 7 a.m. Chaplin's other Royal Mail coaches went via Woburn and Newport Pagnell to Woodside for Liverpool; to Port Patrick via

71   *Another Victorian pub, pictured in August 1940. Local road-sweeper and well-known personality, Sid Davis, who lived nearby in Wolverton Road, chats to two youngsters at the corner of Queen Street.* The Case is Altered *at no.83 was functioning as a pub in 1867 but has long been a private residence.*

Manchester, and to Halifax. It was reported that in three random checks at Stony Stratford in 1794 three Royal Mail guards from Liverpool and Oxford were dismissed for the serious offence of failing to keep their mail boxes locked!

Another reminder of the importance of the town in the old coaching days is given by George Eliot in *Adam Bede*, where Hetty Sorrell takes the coach there on her way to Windsor in search of Captain Donnithorne.

The district had already seen profound changes with the construction of the Grand Junction Canal on the eastern side of the town and the consequent arrival of armies of rough-

and-ready navvies in the neighbourhood, who had come from all parts of the country. A public meeting was held at Stony Stratford on 20 July 1792, but because of the numbers attending it had to be moved from the *Bull* to St Giles church. On completion of the Blisworth tunnel a formal opening ceremony was held on 25 March 1805. A packet boat was ordered for the official party and a dinner provided for 120 people at the *Bull* at a cost of half a guinea each; Mr Praed was in the chair. The dinner started at six o'clock and 'the utmost harmony and conviviality prevailed among the company till near 12 o'clock, when they broke up. All the other

72   *An early photo showing the thatched pub on Horsefair Green first recorded in 1770; the original* Royal Oak *is said to have been a few doors away. The adjacent thatched house was* The Cappers *which is now incorporated in Burnham House — the latter was formerly called The Chestnuts.*

inns in Stony Stratford were filled with company, and many of the parties did not separate till a late hour.'

Fortunately on 18 February 1808 there was only minor local flooding when the aqueduct taking the canal over the river Ouse collapsed. A temporary wooden aqueduct had to be erected, the foundation stone for the stone-work to carry the present 'Iron Trunk' being laid in September 1809: this new aqueduct was opened for traffic in January 1811.

However with the coming of the London and Birmingham railway to Wolverton in 1836, the emphasis of local transport was to

change. Robert Stephenson, the Engineer-in-chief of the line, had begun to stake out the path of the railway in November 1833; despite appalling winter weather conditions it was completed in February. He wrote in January to the secretary of the railway's Birmingham Committee, from the *Cock* at Stony Stratford, 'I have been over the whole of Forster's length with him (i.e. Blisworth to Kilsby tunnel) … The weather is past endurance. I am nearly laid up, having been thoroughly drenched for the last few days …'

What was the effect of the railway on Stony Stratford? Coghlan's *The Iron Road Book* of 1838 had no sympathy with the new situation, stating 'at this time, there cannot be less than 20 inns. How long they will remain inns after the opening of the railroad, requires no ghost from the grave to divine, – serves them right – regular set of fleecers, – open your mouth, and it requires 3s. 6d. to shut it again!' Incidentally another of the railway guides, Joseph Thomas' *Railroad Guide to the London and Birmingham* described how 'The curfew, or eight o'clock bell, is rung here in the winter months, and also a bell at five o'clock in the morning all the year. Until recently, this bell was sounded at four o'clock, but the church-wardens, as the old sexton stated, decided that "four was too early to disturb the inhabitants".'

Hugh Stowell Brown, a Wolverton apprentice who came to know Stony Stratford well during his stay in the district, went on to become a well-respected Baptist minister in Liverpool. He wrote in retrospect of Stony Stratford and Newport Pagnell as towns shorn of their former glories. The railway had superseded the coaches, 'no longer was heard the guard's horn, no longer seen the well-appointed equipages, each with its four fine horses and its proud driver with a bunch of flowers in his button-hole.' The railway folk were looked upon with much disfavour. 'We had ruined the trade of the town.' However, one benefit was that 'most of the wages paid at Wolverton came into the hands of the

73   *The Iron Trunk was completed in 1811; it carried the Grand Junction (later Grand Union) Canal over the Ouse valley and replaced the original aqueduct which had leaked and threatened to flood the valley.*

74 *Referred to as the* Sun *in 1806, the name* Rising Sun *was transferred from the hostelry in London Road, which eventually became the (old)* Plough. *Today it is a private house, 131 High Street, but still noted for its mansard roof. The cart of Mr Mabbutt the carrier stands further along the street in this quiet scene, c.1900; in the distance, right, is the town's gas works.*

Stratford shopkeepers and not less than £100 was spent in the Stratford publics on every Saturday night by the 'station-men', as they were called, yet the talk of the townspeople was full of sad references to the good old coaching days.'

In the last century the roll-call of inns and public-houses that have closed continues to grow. *The Royal Oak* on Horsefair Green has gone and the *Red Lion* in Mill Lane, whilst the old *Plough* in London Road has been demolished. The splendid inn, the *King's Head*, is no longer open at 11 Market Square. *The Barley Mow* (formerly *The Angel*) at 185

High Street, The *Windmill*, no.117 and *The Rising Sun*, no.131 are private houses, while the other *Angel* pub, at no.11, was demolished in the Cofferidge Close development; the rebuilt *White Swan*, no.34, is now a restaurant. Only one of the three public-houses built in Wolverton Road, after the expansion of the town in the 1860s, still functions as such – the *Duke of Wellington*, formerly the *Duke of Edinburgh*. As to the other two, *The Case is Altered* at no.83 is a private house, whilst on the opposite side the *Prince of Wales* at no.68 is an undertaker's business.

Thirteen

EXPLORING THE 1851 CENSUS

Just as there were still many people described as employees of the lace-trade in the villages of North Buckinghamshire – and over 70 people were described as such in Stony Stratford itself – there is increasing evidence in 1851 of the influence of the growing manufacturing industry in the area, arising from the building of the Hayes' works at Stony Stratford and the Wolverton railway works. In addition to the occupations of those

Silver Street, Stony Stratford,

Sep. 1874.

Sir,

I beg most respectfully to inform you that I have been appointed the Town Crier for Stony Stratford in the place of the late Samuel Ashton, deceased, and I should esteem it a favor if you would in future address any bills you might wish to have posted in this Town or Neighbourhood to me. They shall have my prompt and best attention.

I am,

Yours obediently,

THOMAS ELSTONE.

75 *Thomas Elstone's announcement in September 1874 that he has been appointed Town Crier.*

working in the hostelries and taverns and the trades which one would expect to find servicing a country market town, we now come across such jobs as engineer, engine-fitter, smith, boilermaker, striker, turner, smith, white smith, railway labourer and carter at coal wharf.

It is noteworthy how a number of professional men and traders came from distant places to settle in the town and put down their roots. Perhaps at that time, like Wolverton, it might have had the atmosphere of an American frontier town! From the 1851 census we note for example that in the Stratford End of Calverton parish, later known as Calverton End, lived Edwin Forster, the Baptist minister 1836-65, who was to have a very positive influence on the young engineers who travelled on Sundays to be a part of his congregation; he had been born 200 miles away at Stockton-on-Tees. Other 'newcomers' were Edward Hayes and Alexander Collins, both from Manchester; Caroline Wilkins, a shoe binder born at Bloxham, Oxfordshire and Absalom Smith, a shoeing smith from St Albans. From neighbouring villages came William Turney, a grocer and tea dealer born at Cosgrove; John Sleath Gent, a surgeon from Simpson and Thomas Powell, veterinary surgeon born at Newton Longville, whilst natives of the town

Occupations and Trades: 1851 Census, Stony Stratford

agricultural labourers	34	meal dealer	1
banking	2	millers	5
bird & animal stuffer	1	nurses	3
brewers	9	ostlers	3
brickmakers & bricklayers	12	paupers	43
builders	8	pedlars	3
carpenters	9	plumbers, glaziers & painters	15
carriers & draymen	3	portrait painter	1
charwomen	13	postal workers	9
Chelsea pensioner	1	printing	2
chemists	2	property owners	29
clergyman	1	publicans	18
coal merchants	2	railway workers	21
corn-dealer	1	railway works employees	55
dependents 'in work'	10	retail workers	86
dependents	659	retired	4
doctors	3	saddlers	3
domestic servants	111	scholars	218
domestic gardeners	5	shoes	57
domestic grooms	7	skins and leather	2
domestic errand boys	2	straw and baskets	6
dressmakers,		surveyors and auctioneers	3
seamstresses and tailors	57	teachers	13
farmers	4	town crier	1
french polishers	2	transport	4
glover	1	veterinary surgeon	1
grooms	6	watchmaker	1
hairdressers	5	wheelwrights	4
labourers	39	wood manufacturing	9
laceworkers	64		
laundresses and washerwomen	12		
lawyers	6	others, not known	
leather-dealer	1		
manufacturing	10		

76 *James Odell started trading at 60 and 62 High Street in 1863. His shop, Odells Ironmongers and Merchants, was photographed by H.D. Buttrum, c.1895. Note the living accommodation at no.60 where the ground floor was below pavement level. Next door, no.58, was the Post Office at the time, before it moved to no.56.*

included Thomas Downing junior, a blacksmith; Jane Calladine, a shoe manufacturer and Joseph Warren, a currier.

In the parish of Stony Stratford West there were 244 inhabited and 10 uninhabited properties – with two under construction – occupied by 598 males and 658 females. On the west side of the High Street lived William Abraham, designer of lace patterns, born at Kempston; George Back, a surgeon born at Norwich, lived in the house in the High Street, into which Swinfen Harris' parents were to move later from Back Lane. John F. Congreve, attorney, solicitor and superintendent registrar who had been born in Warwickshire, lived at the house later known as St Oswalds and 105 High Street; whilst

natives of the town were William West, a baker and confectioner, and Thomas Worley an attorney, at no.25.

Next door at 23 High Street was George Kightley, a baker and confectioner whose apprentice was George Haseldine, born at Bedford. Further down the street at no.75 was Joseph Howe, chemist and druggist, living with his nephew, a school-boy named William Robinson (both from the village of Milton Keynes), together with Charles Cox, his assistant, who had come from Middlesex. Thus the partnership of William Robinson and Charles Cox founded the firm of Cox & Robinson, which since that time has branched out into the neighbouring counties of Oxfordshire and Northamptonshire, although

77 *The 18th-century chemist's shop of Cox & Robinson at 75 High Street, c.1905. Next door was York House, possibly once the home of York, of Oliver and York's Bank; it was the home of the Slades' York House school for a few years around 1895 before their move to London Road. Today no.77 is the home of the Conservative Club.*

the Stony Stratford headquarters moved subsequently from the High Street to 1 Market Square.

In Church Street was Alfred Hailey, a builder and plumber born at Amersham, whilst of note on the Market Square were William Sharp, a leather merchant from Towcester, and Joseph Hamblin, professor of dancing who had come from London. In Hamblin's household were a groom, two house-servants, three teachers and eight girl students. It is said that Charles Dickens based his character Mr Turveydrop in *Bleak House* on Hamblin. Another important trader at 3-4 Market Square was the master draper, William Boyes, a native of the town. There were also a number of poor people living on the Market Square in small cottages, many of which were to be 'cleared' in the 19th century.

On the western side of the town were also the poorer areas of *White Horse* Yard with 10 houses; Horse Fair with 29 and Cow Fair with 31 houses – these were later named Horsefair Green and Silver Street. Pig Market at the junction with the Market Place had seven more houses and Horn Lane 19 houses.

Coming to the smaller parish of Stony Stratford East, there were 112 inhabited and four uninhabited properties in 1851, with two under construction: these were occupied by 219 males and 282 females. Chapel Street, within which stood the Congregational Chapel, had eight properties. Living there were William Russell, a victualler with two

78 *One of the oldest businesses in the town, Cox &*
Robinson's dates back to 1760. 'Drugs and Chemicals of
the Finest' describes an alcove with four shelves of bottles.
Mr W.P.B. Phillpotts, the owner of the business, is here
displaying an ancient 'Leeches' jar in 1973.

79 *W.R. Mowbray of 7 High Street sold curtain fabrics*
and soft furnishings; in the early 1900s Ralph E. Barley,
the author of Romance around Stony Stratford, *lived*
here. Next door, Hall & White's was an old-style grocery;
the Angel *pub at no.11 had stood there since the late*
1700s. Both the last-named buildings were cleared in the
Cofferidge Close development.

dealers (one from Scotland, the other from Cosgrove) and a Scottish draper.

The eastern side of the High Street as part of the main thoroughfare included many shops. Still recalled today are Henry Tole, the watchmaker born at Newport Pagnell; William Barter, a wharfinger and farmer of 70 acres of land from Hampshire; Frederick Aveline, born at Swanbourne, a carpenter employing three men; two men born in Stony Stratford were John Claridge, master of the National School and Parish Clerk, and John Oliver described as a landowner. Oliver generously bequeathed the interest from £537 Consols to be paid in a yearly subscription of

£3 3s. to the Northampton Infirmary and in equal portions to 20 aged persons of the parish who were regular attendants at the services of duties of the parish church; distribution was to be made at Christmas time.

Listed in 1851 in High Street East as having been born at Northampton was Frances Revill, the wife of an ironmonger employing five men. This shop (62 High Street) was the forerunner of the present Odell's Ironmongers where James Odell commenced trading in 1863. Four years later James Odell was describing himself as a general, furnishing and manufacturing iron-monger and seed merchant, coppersmith, gas-fitter, bell-hanger and brazier. He stocked stoves and ranges, as well as agricultural implements and machines. The present owners, Richard and David Odell, are James's great-grandsons.

At the nearby *Cock Inn* was Mary Chapman, born in Northamptonshire, who had an assistant and seven staff. A grocer, John Attwood Reeve, came from the nearby village of Nash. The last descendant still living in the town of Joseph Valentine, a butcher from Bedford, died only a few years ago. Valentine was proud to advertise in the local newspaper in 1867 that he had purchased a 'portable shop' so that customers could be served at their own homes. Lower down the High Street was William Nixon the printer and stationer, producer of the *Cottage Newspaper*, who hailed from Wisbech, and

John Parrott, an attorney and solicitor, who was born at Aylesbury. Again, the name of Parrott has only recently been lost to the town.

Perhaps Edwin Revill the ironmonger was away from home when the census was taken, but he was a leading townsman and later became proprietor of the *Cock Hotel*. Edwin, 1833-98, was elected the captain of the Stony Stratford fire brigade, which was established in March 1864. One of the best-known men in the town, he was to remain in this post for nearly 35 years. It was said that his assistance was always valuable at Whitsuntide, particularly when a military tournament was part of the Sports held on that occasion. Revill was a member of the yeomanry; indeed he was known as 'Quartermaster Revill' of the Royal Bucks.

80 *Pictured on the left are two buildings in the High Street where the ground floor was below pavement level: a corn shop and the George Hotel. Opposite, on the corner of New Street at 40 High Street, Nimrod C. Benbow had his shop; his sons were later bakers at no.2. Calladine & Son's at no.38 was a long-established boot and shoe-maker.*

81 *Very early view of the* Forester's Arms *in Wolverton Road.*

Hussars. He held the 'medallion' of the St John Ambulance Association and was a churchwarden at St Giles church from 1860.

Back Way was at the rear of the eastern side of the High Street in 1851, with only five properties, but various yards led off High Street east as one came into Stony Stratford from the north. There was Claridge's Lane which had six properties and was to disappear when the St Paul's College complex was built. Then there were Coach and Horses Lane with 12 cottages; the *Bull* Yard with one cottage remaining; Ram Alley with 14; New Street with three, together with three properties lower down the High Street in the old workhouse yard. Ram Alley was to be swept away a decade later with the building of superior properties in New Street when the Rev. Sankey came on the scene.

Still in Wolverton parish in 1851 was the eastern side of what is now London Road. There were six old cottages standing next to where the church was to be built just over a decade later. William Cowley, born at Newport Pagnell, a bricklayer who employed six men, lived in this area, as well as local 'character', Adam Sherwood the chimney-sweep, born at Cosgrove, more of whom later. These cottages, belonging to the Radcliffe Trust, were taken down at the end of the century.

William Barter at the old *Plough Inn*, London Road, and Benjamin Barter, the miller at Wolverton mill were both 'locals', being natives of Wolverton. There were also various agricultural workers living in that area of the town, no doubt working for the tenant-farmers who occupied the farms in the guardianship of the Radcliffe Trust.

Unfortunately the entries for both New and Old Wolverton in 1851 were not listed in any systematic order. For example, whilst 13 entries representing 74 persons specifically relate to the parish house, other entries were interspersed amongst them. The Debbs Barn house, which after the 1939-45 War was to give its name to the area of council housing on the approach to Stony Stratford from Wolverton, was at that time only occupied by a gardener and his family, while a toll-collector still lived at the 'Wolverton Gate' nearby. By this time workers' cottages had been built also at Slated Row, Old Wolverton. In the Milton Keynes of the 21st century it is easy to forget that in 1851 there were working farms extending from Manor Farm in the north to Stacey Hill Farm in the south and from Stonebridge Farm in the east to Brick Kiln Farm in the west.

Fourteen

HISTORIC BUILDINGS

Today some of the larger houses have gone, most of their coach-houses have been converted and their paddocks built over. Thus the face of the town has continued to change, if only in a gradual manner. Historic Stony Stratford is a small area, so any loss diminishes the stock of older, historic, properties. The remaining important private house is 48 High Street, which has a shell-hooded porch; it is a William and Mary dwelling of the 1690s with timber-framing at the rear. Until the 1930s, it boasted an Elizabethan stable, which was demolished when the back gardens in New Street were slightly enlarged.

At the corner of High Street and Church Street next to St Giles Church was a timber-framed shop dating from the 16th century but later rebuilt, known locally as the 'Donkey Shop', literally because the owner kept a donkey! This interesting property was demolished in the widening of the entrance to Church Street before the Second World War. It was also one of those places where one had to go down steps to the ground-floor level. The house at 60 High Street, replaced by Odell's modern showroom, was another example, as well as the corn-shop by the *Old George*; the latter itself is one of the few surviving properties with this feature. One can speculate that the *Old George* was

82 *Walter Yates with family and friends outside his chandler's shop, 39 High Street, c.1902. This was a property where one went down steps into the shop.*

83   *The* George Hotel, *shown here c.1900 and first recorded early in the 17th century, is one of the few buildings in the town today reached by steps down to the ground floor. At the back of the property was the smithy of Walter Holland, until the Health Centre was built. The* George Yard *was* The Hobby *that led to paths across the fields and the river to Passenham.*

84   *The* White House *in Wolverton Road, after conversion into a bus station and the offices of the United Counties Omnibus Company. These were brought into use on 28 August 1955.*

perhaps a larger property, the lane known as the Hobby running by its side.

Gone also is the ancient stone dwelling-house at the corner of Swan Terrace and Russell Street known as Stratford Place. In the middle of the 19th century the *Swan* had horses and traps for hire; James Cross' omnibus went from *The Chequers* at Newport Pagnell twice in the morning to Wolverton and Stony Stratford. *The Swan* was rebuilt early in 1915.

The new Catholic church of St Mary Magdalene was built in 1958 on the garden site of another large old house, St Oswald's, but the church was set back from the old street-line. St Oswald's, occupied in 1830 by

85 *Programme of films being shown in February 1935 at the Palace Cinema, Wolverton and the Scala Cinema in Wolverton Road, (telephone number Stony Stratford 94). There was a continuous performance every evening from 6 p.m., with the added attraction of a spacious free car park!*

THE PALACE

MONDAY, FEBRUARY 4th, for three evenings
"THE CHURCH MOUSE"
Starring LAURA LA PLANTE and IAN HUNTER
A great Comedy full of hearty laughs

THURSDAY, FEBRUARY 7th, for three evenings
"STAMBOUL QUEST"
Starring MYRNA LOY and GEORGE BRENT
A thrilling spy romance

MONDAY, FEBRUARY 11th, for three evenings
"TREASURE ISLAND"
Starring WALLACE BEERY and JACKIE COOPER
Robert Louis Stevenson's immortal story. The greatest adventure story ever written

THURSDAY, FEBRUARY 14th, for three evenings
"MY SONG FOR YOU"
Starring JAN KIEPURA and SONNIE HALE The golden voiced Jan Kiepura in a gay and sparkling musical picture

MONDAY, FEBRUARY 18th, for three evenings
"BORN TO BE BAD" Starring Loretta Young and Cary Grant
The story of a very modern girl And
"SILENT MEN" Starring TIM McCOY A thrilling Western picture

THURSDAY, FEBRUARY 21st, for three evenings
"LILIES OF THE FIELD"
Starring Winifred Shotter, Anthony Bushell & Claude Hulbert
A British comedy

MONDAY, FEBRUARY 25th, for three evenings
"JEW SUSS" Starring Conrad Veidt with Benita Hume, Sir Gerald Du Maurier, Frank Vosper and Cedric Hardwicke
A great novel—now a great film you'll never forget

THURSDAY, FEBRUARY 28th, for three evenings
"MADAME DU BARRY" Starring DELORES DEL RIO
The most dazzling romance of the age. Intimate secrets exposed
The one show you've been waiting for is here

THE SCALA

MONDAY, FEBRUARY 4th, for three evenings
"LOOKING FOR TROUBLE"
Starring SPENCER TRACY and JACK OAKIE
The new kings of comedy in a riot of laughter

THURSDAY, FEBRUARY 7th, for three evenings
"SERVANTS ENTRANCE"
Starring JANET GAYNOR and LEW AYRES
Her latest success

MONDAY, FEBRUARY 11th, for three evenings
Commencing these three evenings at 5.45 p.m.
"DR. MONICA"
Starring KAY FRANCIS with 4 great stars in a great story
and **"DANCING FOOL"** Starring HAL LE ROY
Laughs, song and fun—a riot of youth and melody

THURSDAY, FEBRUARY 14th, for three evenings
"TREASURE ISLAND"
Starring WALLACE BEERY and JACKIE COOPER
Robert Louis Stevenson's greatest adventure story
A real treat for young and old

MONDAY, FEBRUARY 18th, for three evenings
"STRAIGHT IS THE WAY"
Starring FRANCHOT TONE and MAY ROBSON
A crook melodrama
and **"LEST WE FORGET"** Starring Stewart Rome
in a lesson in loyalty

THURSDAY, FEBRUARY 21st, for three evenings
Commencing these three evenings at 5.45 p.m.
"GIRLS PLEASE"
Starring SYDNEY HOWARD and JANE BAXTER
See Sydney in his funniest picture
and **"DANGEROUS CROSSROADS"**
A romantic and thrilling action drama

MONDAY, FEBRUARY 25th, for three evenings
"THE DRAGON MURDER CASE"
Starring WARREN WILLIAM and MARGARET LINDSAY
The most baffling of all murder mysteries
and **"THE OFFICE WIFE"**
Starring DOROTHY BOUCHIER and NORA SWINBURNE
A merry British comedy

THURSDAY, FEBRUARY 28th, for three evenings
"JEW SUSS"
Starring CONRAD VEIDT and a big all star cast
A great novel—now a great film

86 *At one time the Market Square boasted of many inns. In this view, c.1910, no.8 Market Square, the Working Men's Club until 1948, had earlier been the* White Hart, *first recorded in 1625; no.9, recorded in 1666, is today still the* Crown; *no.10, a butcher's, was formerly the* Barley Mow *from about 1770; the agent of the Northampton Brewery Company was at no.7.*

a solicitor, John Freer Congreve, was subsequently a doctor's home until the death of Dr Douglas Bull, who had followed his father Colonel William Bull into the practice. Father and son were both leading figures in the town.

Moving on to Wolverton Road, when the White House, which had been designed in the Italianate style, was bought by the United Counties bus company, the house inevitably became its local offices, although regrettably it was demolished eventually to make way for a modern bus station and garage. Such are the winds of change nowadays that these new facilities too became the victims of 'progress' or asset-stripping, being dem-

olished to make way for the Emerton Gardens housing development. The Lodge to the White House went even earlier: it had stood on the left-hand side of what became the forecourt of the adjacent *Scala Cinema*, a building which later rejoiced in the name of a tyre firm, 'Fred the Tread'. A photograph of the 1950s shows a display-cabinet for stills that advertised the current films, standing where the Lodge had been. Another 19th-century property, York House in London Road, said to have been built for a banker, was an imposing building for its time but the structure now needs some attention and its setting has deteriorated. In the 1881 Census the White House was shown as

87   *Houses near St Giles church, c.1920: 1 and 3 Church Street were demolished to widen the entrance road into Church Street from the High Street; whilst 5 and 7 Church Street were cleared more than 30 years later to make way for the County Library.*

88 *A good view of Jeff's House on the Market Square, c.1905, unfortunately demolished in 1908.*

Ellentree House; a former name for York House was Clarence House.

As a general point, although the Donkey shop and Stratford Place, together with the Elizabethan stables of 48 High Street, were demolished pre-1939 and other pleasant properties after the war in slum-clearance and road-widening under the Town and Country Planning Acts' powers of compulsory purchase, a more sympathetic regime came into play in the late 1960s, when the Milton Keynes Development Corporation was established.

During its existence historic buildings were treated more sympathetically; consideration was given to new uses for old buildings and any conversions were carried out with greater awareness of the past. The Corporation showed the way with the appointment of a Conservation Officer; one ideal of the time was that the villages of Milton Keynes would be conserved and integrated into the development, in a similar fashion to the old villages that have been drawn into the metropolis of London.

Fifteen

THE BUILDING PARSONS AND PARISH LIFE

The Rev. Campbell Christie, vicar of St Giles 1851-9, was the first of the so-called 'building parsons' and he began by building Calverton House as his vicarage on part of Higlin's Piece on the western side of Calverton Road off Horsefair Green. Later, Calverton House was a doctor's residence; when this ceased it was turned into apartments. Today the house stands rather forlorn, most of its grounds utilised for the post-war housing expansion in Ousebank Way. The Rev. Christie was also responsible for converting the old Bell Rope Charity acre in Calverton Road into a cemetery, where two gothic-style mortuary chapels were erected about 1856. These Anglican and Protestant chapels were demolished after the Second World War, the spaces being utilised for cremation burials.

89 *Planning a Conservative Party fête in Higlin's Piece along Calverton Road; left to right are Police Sergeant Rollings, Special Constable Mackerness, Lord Denham, Major Whiteley and the Conservative Agent Hazell. In the background stands the water tower on the corner of Augustus Road; two bungalows have since replaced it.*

Christie's successor was the Rev. William Thompson Sankey 1859-75, who proved to be a great benefactor to the town. He was instrumental in clearing away many slum buildings to make way for two blocks of houses on either side of New Street. (The dates of these buildings were cast in the hoppers at the head of the down-water pipes.)

The terrace on the northern side, commencing with 3 New Street, is of 1862 by the architect Henry Woodyer; these buildings are three-storeyed. On the southern side opposite, a block of single-storey dwellings is flanked on either side by a two-storey house, the smaller houses giving the impression that they are almshouses. Interestingly the initials of the vicar and his wife and the date of building are worked into the brickwork of the gables of the two flanking houses, as W.T. & J.S. 1863. There is also a curious cottage of a similar date at the Vicarage Road end, no.24, to which a small kitchen was added to give more space some years ago.

New Street progressed down to the Vicarage, also built for Sankey 1860-1: this was demolished in 1971 although the site was put to good use as a residential home for the elderly. Another house similar in style to the New Street houses and dated 1866 is 99 Wolverton Road. Although the original connection with Sankey has not been determined, we know that in 1881 it was tenanted by someone who worked at St Paul's College.

In fact Sankey's *pièce-de-résistance* was the college, built 1863-5 in the High Street between the old Pudding Bag Lane and Coach

90   *The Rev. William Sankey, vicar of St Giles, 1859-75.*

and Horses Lane. Sankey was its founder and warden from January 1864, the Rev. Richard Winkfield the headmaster. Students had a classical education. One of the old boys was George Grossmith, well-known for *The Diary of a Nobody* and for a part in the original production of Gilbert and Sullivan's opera *The Sorcerer*. He was the son of a journalist; the Harmsworths, who were also students, went into journalism.

There was room for 200 boarders; most paid fees of 24 guineas a year but 12 'foundation boys' paid half that amount. Space was

91 *W.T. Sankey's vicarage of 1860-1, shown here in the winter of 1904, became redundant after the Rev. Cavell-Northam chose to live in the former St Mary's vicarage in London Road. The old vicarage was thus demolished, making way for St Giles Mews today.*

92 *Wall-paintings in the chapel of St Paul's College. The Rev. Sankey arrived as vicar of Stony Stratford in 1859. Wealthy and energetic, he had the College built at a total cost of £40,000.*

reserved also for 12 apprentice servitors who received three hours of lessons every day and were required to assist in the work of the house: they paid £5 each per annum. There was a Spartan regime; morning roll-call was at 5.45 a.m., an hour later in winter. Work began at once with a break for breakfast at 7 a.m. and another at 10.30 a.m., after which lessons went on until one o'clock. Games were played after lunch behind the school on the four-acre field. Lessons then resumed from six o'clock until 8.30 p.m.; lights-out was at 9.15 p.m.

93 *All Fegan's Homes boys were given jobs; here a boy is cutting the grass.*

The history of the St Paul's complex has been described in detail elsewhere: firstly, it was an Anglican college until 1880 and then from 1882-95; briefly a cigar factory in 1896, after which it closed for four years. However in 1900 the buildings were purchased as a boys' orphanage of a strictly nonconformist persuasion by Mr J.W.C. Fegan. There was a home for younger boys at Yardley Gobion, and a working farm at Goudhurst in Kent. Some of the boys were to immigrate to Canada after their time at the orphanage, up to the outbreak of the Second World War.

When in 1962 Fegan's Homes closed at Stony Stratford the premises became a Franciscan catholic preparatory school. However that ceased operations in 1972; the next occupant was a Swiss bank, Société Générale. When that also ended, there was a feeling that some community use should be found for the extensive buildings. Regrettably, this did not materialise; today the old college buildings are split into a number of 'desirable' houses and other units, with a restaurant operating in the former chapel. The swimming-pool was filled in; a block of

94   *On the left, c.1920, is a lesser-known building, 99 Wolverton Road of 1866, which has all the features of Sankey's buildings. We know that an employee of St Paul's College lived there in 1881.*

95   *An earlier choir screen in St Giles church, c.1900, painted with panels portraying the saints. This in turn was replaced in 1905 by the screen that was destroyed in the fire of Boxing Day 1964.*

96 *Sunday-morning service in St Mary and St Giles church, after its restoration. The choir is in the gallery at the west end; the Rev. C. Cavell-Northam is in the aisle to the right, whilst prominent parishioners are Ron Odell kneeling on extreme left; Mr and Mrs Riley, two seats behind him and Miss Maggie Yates, on the outside, third row in the left-hand aisle.*

retirement homes called Fegan's Court was built at the rear of the property. In addition the playing field, further to the rear, was used to extend the Ancell Trust sports ground.

On his arrival in the area the Rev. Sankey lived at Wolverton House for a short time. In his early years as vicar he organised many talks of an educational nature for his parishioners as well as concerts and entertainment at the National schoolroom in the High Street. His wife was instrumental in arranging a sale of ladies' handiwork in aid of

the new parsonage building fund, held from 11-13 April 1861. Later, there was a suitable celebration when the vicarage was opened on 24 June 1861, at which a number of important persons from the local aristocracy and gentry were present, including relatives of the Duke of Grafton from Wakefield Lawn.

Sankey arranged for allotments of 10-20 poles in size to be established in the cottage garden, adjoining the parsonage field. The gardeners were to pay one shilling a pole quarterly in advance. To publicise this new

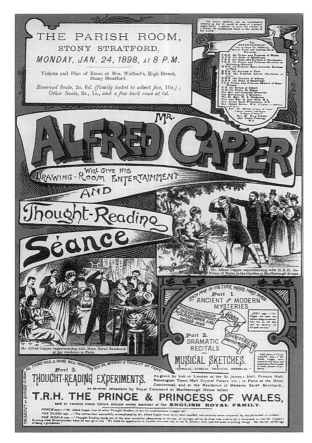

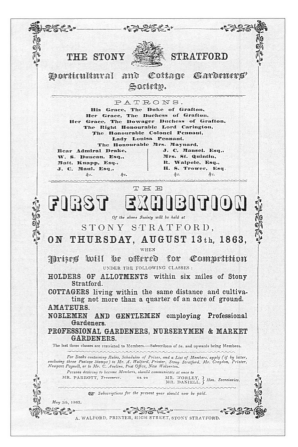

97 & 98   Left: *One of the most interesting, unique entertainments took place in St Giles Parish Room in New Street on 24 January 1898 when Alfred Capper, the renowned thought-reader, paid a repeat visit to the town and under the heading of 'Ancient and Modern Mysteries' held an audience captive with his many experiments.* Right: *The first of many exhibitions for gardeners to display their prize exhibits was held on 13 August 1863.*

enterprise, a first show of garden produce from the Cottage allotments took place in June 1862.

By 1861 there were a number of parish organisations in existence. There were church societies such as the Sunday Schools, the Church Missionary society, a parochial association for the Society for the Propagation of the Gospel as well as the Bible Society. In addition there was an Evening School in the winter months for men and boys and a

Savings Bank at noon on Mondays for an hour with a Coal Club from June to November from 11 a.m.-1 p.m. Then a Clothing Club was held at noon on alternate Wednesdays with a lending library on Sundays after the afternoon service and also for an hour on Mondays. A soup kitchen was open on Fridays during the winter months.

A number of charities were extant in 1861. One of these, the Blue Coat charity, had been endowed by Sir Simon Bennett in 1631 for clothing the poor men of St Giles parish. Rents from Sir Simon's Bradwell charity were expended in providing work for poor men. Similarly from 1670 there was Whalley's charity for apprenticing boys, whilst from 1691 Dr Arnold's charity supplied money relief to the poor who attended church and did not receive parochial relief; there was a further sum for binding apprentices.

Whitwell's Bread Charity distributed 40 loaves every Sunday to the poor attending church. The Street Charity made various bequests, which were applied to cleansing, paving and lighting the parish. Another charity was the Bell-Rope where, after the furnishing of bell-ropes, the balance of the bequest was applied to general church purposes. Lastly in the list of charitable institutions of the parish was 'The Female Friendly Society. Established in 1803. Secretary, Mrs J. Smith'.

On 20 January 1863 the building opened at the New Street-Vicarage Road corner, supplied by the Rev. Sankey himself as a Parish Room for St Giles and a 'handsome Infant School': the latter was for children aged two to seven years living in the town and neighbourhood, for a payment of one penny per week.

The Rev. Sankey was very active in his parish: he was president of the Stony Stratford Amateur Musical Society in 1862. Its patrons were the Duchess of Grafton and her daughter-in-law, the Countess Euston. A Musical Society was formed for the 'practice of vocal and instrumental music'. Sankey was also President of the Literary Institution. An annual festival of parish choirs had been started in 1861, drawing in choirs from Stony Stratford and neighbouring places, such as

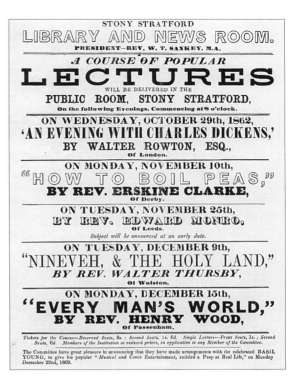

99 *The Rev. Sankey was President of the Library and News Room which met in the Public Room. Lectures were on a variety of topics, usually given by clerical gentlemen. What was the secret of 'How to boil peas' in 1862?*

100 *The Rev. William Pitt Trevelyan, Rector of Calverton, who with Lady Mary Russell and the Radcliffe Trust were the chief benefactors in building the church of Wolverton St Mary in 1864. Photograph, c.1880.*

101 *The area of London Road influenced by the Rev. W.P. Trevelyan. On the left, part of St Mary's church, its parish being formed on 29 November 1870; right, the front block of Calverton Limes 1870 by E.S. Harris. Granny Beard from no.32 is wearing an ankle-length skirt, a cape and cap. Telegraph poles were then notable features along Watling Street.*

Bradwell, Calverton, Cosgrove, Deanshanger, Fenny Stratford, Hanslope, Haversham, Loughton, Willen, Newport Pagnell, Passenham, Walton, Wavendon and Woolstone. The vicar was also secretary of a group of the local clergy, whilst on 'home ground' he even diligently set about the re-seating of St Giles church in 1864.

The third of the building parsons was the Rev. William Pitt Trevelyan, who was rector of Calverton from 1859 to 1881 and vicar of Old Wolverton from 1856 to 1871. He began to develop the lower end of London Road, part of the new ecclesiastical parish of Wolverton St Mary, and made a further impact by contributing to the building of St Mary's church and the church schools. The Rev. Trevelyan was instrumental with John Worley and others in inaugurating the Stony Stratford Dispensary and the Cottage Hospital, although the latter eventually was discontinued, being replaced by a Hospital Fund. Trevelyan's son, the Rev. George P. Trevelyan, was vicar of St Mary's from 1885. Another magnificent property in the area was the present Working Men's Club, built for the surgeon William C. Daniell, where W.P. Trevelyan later lived.

Sixteen

HAYES BOATYARD

Stony Stratford was the most unlikely place for sea-going vessels to be built, yet it was there that tugs, launches and other boats were built by the firm of Edward Hayes. After completion, a vessel would be drawn behind a traction engine from the Hayes' works near the brow of the hill in London Road, northwards down London Road, along the High Street and over the causeway and the Ouse Bridge into Wharf Lane at Old Stratford. There is one recorded instance, however, in 1906, where a team of six horses took the tug *Irurukbat* as far as the entrance to Wharf Lane. As vessels lay at the wharf the engines were fitted, last adjustments were made and then, the funnel and deck fitments dismantled, boats were ready for launching sideways down a greasy wooden ramp on to the Grand Junction Canal.

They were then prepared for the long and often difficult journey down the inland waterway to the Thames. Some went to London; others joined the Kennet and Avon canal to make their way to Bristol. Larger boats, fitted out at Brentford, took to the sea: one sailed to Hull and then across country by canal to Liverpool. Others hugged the English coast to the ports, whilst a few ventured quite safely on the high seas. Some were transported overseas on larger vessels.

The first Edward Hayes, 1818-77, hailed from Manchester and went as an apprentice to the Wolverton works of the London & Birmingham Railway, which was then managed by the Loco. Superintendent, Edward Bury, who himself was a partner in the Clarence Foundry of Liverpool. Hayes lodged in a cottage at Old Wolverton with three other young men from 1840 to 43. The Rev. Hugh Stowell Brown as a young man had been one of this group of four youngsters: he quaintly described their landlord at one point as 'a peasant called Cox'! From 1847-50 Hayes is recorded as the Master at the British and Foreign School which stood at the corner of the High Street and Wolverton Road in Stony Stratford. He married a local girl, but still throughout his life maintained links with his birthplace.

By 1851 Hayes was described as a consulting engineer and the superintendent of a college, living at 8 Horsefair Green; consequently his business seems to have been established about 1850, rather than the date of 1840 that the firm's note-paper declared some 80 years later! Next, Hayes established himself as an agricultural engineer at the Watling Works in London Road. In 1857 he was listed as one of the trustees of the Baptist chapel, which was to be built at New Bradwell.

EDWARD HAYES, ENGINEER,
WATLING WORKS, STONEY STRATFORD, BUCKS.

PATENTEE OF IMPROVEMENTS FOR MARINE ENGINES.
PATENTEE OF WINDLASS FOR STEAM PLOUGHING,

Which obtained the Silver Medal at the Royal Agricultural Show, Leeds, July, 1861, and Honourable Mention was made of the Portable Engine and Windlass at the International Exhibition, 1862.

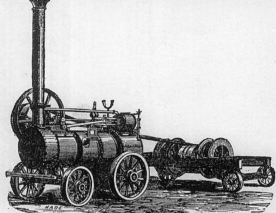

First.—This Windlass is constructed so as to use with advantage the simple and ordinary portable engine with one cylinder, and so employ much of the capital already expended in the Steam Engine for agricultural purposes.

Second. — No windlass-man is required; one man superintends both engine and windlass.

Third.—The anchor-man at each headland stops the implement without stopping the engine.

Fourth.— The work can be done in fogs, or by Moonlight in the harvest month, with perfect safety to the Machinery.

Fifth.—No wheels are required to be put in or out of gear.

OPINIONS OF THE PRESS:—

The TIMES, July 17th, 1861.	The ENGINEER, July 19th, 1861.	LEEDS MERCURY, July 15th, 1861.
Mr. HAYES, of Stoney Stratford, exhibited a very clever windlass on the coiling principle.	The self-acting windlass of Mr. EDWARD HAYES, of Stoney Stratford, was one of the most important novelties in the show.	As a piece of mechanism this deserves as much attention as anything in the field,

This Establishment receives Young Gentlemen as Pupils, who are trained in Mechanical Engineering. For Prospectuses apply as above. See also description of Stoney Stratford.

102   *By 1861 Edward Hayes senior was making his mark with agricultural innovations and moving into marine work. Illustrated is his self-acting windlass with details of its benefits.*

In that same year Hayes patented a self-acting windlass; he received a silver medal from the Royal Agricultural Society Leeds in 1861. The original foundry in London Road was replaced, as it proved to be too small. Thus the works expanded and by the 1860s some 60 mechanics were engaged in the manufacture of steam engines and general machinery; there were also 25 pupils.

Hayes built up fine rapport with other engineering colleagues in the district, such as James Edward McConnell, who succeeded Bury as locomotive superintendent of the London & North Western Railway's works at Wolverton. The name L.N.W.R. arose after the London & Birmingham railway merged with other railway companies. Also living at one time in Stony Stratford was Thomas Rickett, another ex-Wolverton apprentice, who aroused Hayes' interest by going on to manufacture steam cars at the Castle Foundry in Buckingham;

103 *Hayes works, c.1910, before the days of Health and Safety! The shafting, a linked system of pulleys and belts, drove the machinery.*

a further innovator was William Smith of Little Woolstone, who was renowned for his cultivator. Hayes was also on good terms with the local gentry and clergy. This was in evidence at a large gathering in 1862, when the Rev. Sankey showed that he held Hayes in great respect as someone who practised 'practical Christianity'. Sankey emphasised also that he was pleased to find that Hayes had recovered recently from a severe illness.

Hayes replied that when he had first attempted to establish an evening school in the town, he had encountered many difficulties and was called many hard names. Some persons had said he was an infidel; one old woman said that he was a 'stationer' and that she did not like stationers. In this manner the lady was referring to the fact that Hayes had worked at 'Wolverton Station' (New Wolverton's earlier name). 'He was a far-comer and she did not like far-comers. He

104 *A traction engine has just brought a tug for launching on the canal at Hayes Wharf, the building on the left. Work is in progress on a motor-launch, the* Susi. *Its funnel has not been lowered, so presumably it is not yet ready for the journey to London.*

was a railway man and she did not like railways or Lucifer matches, both of which she regarded as inventions of the devil. Lucifer matches, she said, were invented to enable thieves to steal and the railway was invented to enable them to get their goods away': thus it appeared that distrust of the newcomer was a factor just as prevalent in 19th-century Stony Stratford, as it has been more recently in the evolution of the new town of Milton Keynes.

At that time Hayes hoped that he would have success in the experiments he was conducting to apply steam-power to boats upon the canal. By 1864 he was described as an engineer and patentee and manufacturer of steam-ploughing machinery, whilst his engineering establishment at the south end of the town was for the training of young men from respectable families, as mechanical engineers.

His son, Edward junior 1845-1917, was born at Stony Stratford; he was a pupil of his father for some four to five years from 1863. In his youth Edward rode to hounds; his other leisure pursuits were skating, fishing, shooting and croquet. He married twice: his first wife, whom he married in 1876, died 30 years later, but he remarried in 1908. In later life he was a member of the Stony Stratford Rural District Council and the Potterspury Workhouse Board of Guardians. At one time it was thought that Hayes had built the house named 'Mansfield' next to St Mary's church, but documentation has been found that he was initially a tenant, and did not purchase the property until 1895.

At the beginning of his career, Hayes II gained experience of the construction of small steam vessels and machinery on the river Weaver; he experimented also with light craft vessels on canals and on the river at Leamington. He became manager of the Watling Works in 1869 and subsequently its owner, on his father's death.

In the *Illustrated London News* of 20 January 1877 is a description of a flat-bottomed barge supplied by Hayes to Manchester Corporation. This was designed especially for the carriage of 100 boxes, each containing half a ton of manure; in effect the city's treated household sewage. The barge had a derrick crane in the centre, by

105 Douro*, pictured at Old Stratford, was a tug completed in August 1902; it made its trial trip from Lennox Wharf on Millwall Pier to Gravesend Hospital on 4 September 1902. It was 52ft. 6in. long with a draft of 4ft.*

106   *The only known illustration of* The Worker, *following its launch in October 1915. It was ordered for the Imperial Russian Ministry of Trade and Industries at Petrograd for work at Archangel and was shipped there on board the S.S.* Meridian.

which the boxes were unloaded, and measured 68ft. long, 14ft. wide, and 5ft. 6in. deep; the displacement of water was only 3ft. 6in. In all it was said to be a great credit to its engineer, in this new enterprise of the Corporation!

In the same year *Kelly's Directory* listed Hayes as a maker of steam tugs for canals and rivers, steam yachts and launches, portable stationary and traction engines and travelling anchors. He was patentee of the latter and of the steam-cultivating windlass. Hayes constructed marine engines and small steam vessels up to about 80ft. in length, chiefly screw vessels, built of steel and in great variety. Numbers of these, stern-wheelers and

107 Aileen *is seen in a commercial postcard view on the Grand Union Canal at Old Wolverton. Ordered in May 1923 by Sena Sugar Estates for use at Chinde in Portuguese East Africa, it was 51ft. long, 12ft. wide with a 4ft. 6in. draft. Because it ran into difficulties going along the Cosgrove Arm of the canal, 'the assistance of horses was required'.*

paddle boats, were sent abroad. In 1869, a steam yacht won the International Race at Argenteuil; in the same year the firm took honours at the French Exhibition for its design of steamers for the Metropolitan Fire Brigade.

The Board of Works and the London County Council engaged Hayes to build steam tugs for the Thames. His vessels, which also included motor launches, towing launches and yachts, were built for prominent organisations both in this country and overseas. A random selection would include the *John Brown* of 1883, for Sierra Leone; the *Pioneer* of 1891, going to Axim, West Africa; the *Curlew* of 1903 for Cape Town; and the *Suzette* of 1904

which was for the Sultan of Morocco. In 1907 the *Crown* went to Trinidad and the *Lautaro* to Chile. Two years later, the *Ramtirth* was bought by an Indian chief, the *Etienne Watel* by the Compagnie des Mines de Senegambia. The *Popular* of 1910 was for Portugal and the *Vigilant* for Brazil; *The Worker* was built for use at Archangel in Russia, 1915. The *AS161* was destined for French canals; on home rivers, the *Mercie* of 1913 went to the Tees; the *Pat* to the Thames in 1923. The *Pat*, today re-engined and renamed *Wey*, is still in existence.

By 1914 the Company had representation at Westminster in London. Many trials of vessels took place on the Thames. During

108 *Boats undertook proving trial runs on the Thames before they went on their way to their purchasers. Here a vessel has passed under Westminster Bridge, close to the familiar landmark of County Hall, with electric trams running over the bridge. Hayes' London office was nearby.*

the war it was thought that upwards of 50 Hayes' steamers were engaged in the conflict, some of them hunting U-boats.

Records of the company are very hard to find today. Wages listed for just one week, at the end of January 1891, show that four smiths, working 56 to 62 hours, received between £1 0s. 1d. and £1 16s. 8d. and 14 fitters, working 35½ to 56 hours, earned wages varying from 4s. 3d. ;to £1 14s. 6d. One carpenter earned 15s. 4d. for 20½ hours, another £1 3s. 10d. for 54 hours. Twelve boat-builders, working from 48¾ to 53¾ hours, were paid from 5s. 0d. to £1 14s. 3d. Five boilermakers obtained 5s. 8d. to £5 1s. 7d. for 38 to 52 hours: this larger amount included a 'special payment'. Two pupils, designated labourers, earned 8d. and 1s. 4d. each; lastly, four 'miscellaneous' workers received respectively 5s., 13s., 14s. 4d. and £1 10s.

When Edward junior died in 1917, his elder son Arthur, also known as Edward, took over the business. A Member of the Institution of Naval Architects, he was also a freemason, a follower of the Bucks. Otter Hounds, a keen angler and fly-fisher, but he is said not to have taken any prominent part in the organisations of the town. On Arthur's premature death in 1920, the firm became Edward Hayes Ltd; its directors were E.H. Littledale, a former Hayes pupil; Archie Bates, a former Hayes foreman and R.C. Erridge. One of their specialities was the light-draft steamer made in sections for re-erection abroad. If any vessel was too large to launch on the canal at Old Stratford, it was built with every section marked and then dismantled for re-assembly.

109 *The last surviving tug today is believed to be the* Pat. *Ordered in December 1923 by Mr Beckett of Kingston upon Thames, it is passing Cox & Robinson's shop in the High Street on its way for launching at Old Stratford. Built for use on the Thames, it was 45ft. long, 11ft. wide with a 5ft. 2in. draft.*

Despite the closure of the boat-building yard about 1925, many of the craft continued in service, requests for spare parts being received at the London Road Garage even in the 1960s. The last boat to be built is believed to have been *Sparteolus, c.*1925. So came to an end this curious enterprise of a small boat-building works in an inland location.

Seventeen

EDWARD SWINFEN HARRIS, ARCHITECT

The architect Edward Swinfen Harris was a Stony Stratford man who left his mark, particularly in North Buckinghamshire and South Northamptonshire. He was born on 30 July 1841 at 36 High Street, which until the 1960s was still a private house. Edward was the eldest son of E.S. Harris senior, the clerk to the Stony Stratford bench of magistrates, to the Board of Guardians, and to the Hockliffe & Stony Stratford and Buckingham & Newport Pagnell Turnpike Trusts.

The young Swinfen, as he was called, is said to have developed at an early age a talent for drawing and an interest in heraldry, which stood him in good stead in his career. The Harris's moved later to Back Lane. At about 11 years of age Swinfen went to the Belvidere

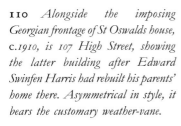

110 *Alongside the imposing Georgian frontage of St Oswalds house, c.1910, is 107 High Street, showing the latter building after Edward Swinfen Harris had rebuilt his parents' home there. Asymmetrical in style, it bears the customary weather-vane.*

III   *An assortment of period furniture and photographs decorates one of the rooms of Swinfen Harris's house in the 1890s. Servants would have been summoned by the bell-handle on the wall, left.*

Academy at Old Stratford. There the Rev. John Thomas prepared boys for public schools and universities. Later Swinfen boarded at Ullathorpe House School in Leicestershire; in about 1858 he was apprenticed in the book trade, but left to become articled to an architect in London.

On completion of his articles, he shared an office with two friends in London. In 1867 he designed additions to the parish church of St Nicholas, Tooting Graveney, Wandsworth and the next year returned to Stony Stratford to make additions to Wolverton St Mary vicarage and Calverton Limes in the London Road. Later he worked on the new churches of Holloway Emmanuel, London, with F.R. Farrow in 1878-9; Clifford's Mesne St Peter, Gloucestershire 1880-2; St Margaret's Mission

Church at Fenny Stratford 1885-6, and Mortimer St John, Berkshire in 1894-7. In addition he built extensions and restored a number of churches throughout the country, and also worked on the Eglise Anglicaine at Dieppe.

On and off for many years he was engaged with a number of churches around Stony Stratford. As well as the two churches in his home town, he worked on Holy Trinity at Old Wolverton, Wolverton St George's, Calverton All Saints, Loughton All Saints and Bradwell St Laurence. Other Buckinghamshire churches where he worked, include those at Moulsoe, Bow Brickhill, Lillingstone Dayrell and Hardmead, together with Cosgrove, Deanshanger, Furtho, Paulerspury and Wicken in Northamptonshire.

112 *No.5 High Street, c.1910. Beyond Canvin the butcher and Meadows the outfitter was another Swinfen Harris house with a weathervane; here it is pictured before its conversion to a shop.*

Swinfen travelled extensively, mostly on architectural tours; in the course of these trips he visited most parts of France as well as Germany, Italy, Belgium, Austria and a small part of Spain. He had started married life near Stony Stratford at Potterspury in 1870, but it was not long before he moved back to 15 Wolverton Road, Stony Stratford. His first completely new building was the school at

Grafton Regis in 1873, followed by the social club and school at Yardley Gobion. He was county surveyor for North Buckinghamshire 1875-89; one of his projects in this job was the bridge at Sherington. Following the passing of the Education Act, Swinfen built a number of schools such as those at Adstock, Beachampton (now named Teal House), Mursley and Tingewick. His

St Mary's School at Stony Stratford is the present *Plough* inn. He also worked at Stony Stratford mill.

His distinctive style of domestic architecture can be seen in Stony Stratford at 5 High Street and at 19 Wolverton Road, the latter built for Dr Paddy Maguire. Another doctor's home was *The Elms* in Green Lane, Wolverton. At Newport Pagnell three of his works were *Lovat Bank*, the home of businessman Mr Taylor in Silver Street; Church Cottage, close to the parish church;

and 2 Union Street. Another work not far away was the rectory at Maids Moreton.

On the death of his father in 1887, Swinfen's mother turned the family home over to him, with an adjoining cottage, which he reconstructed to his own design as the present 107 High Street. He lived there from 1892 until his death on 30 May 1924, his wife predeceasing him in 1918. He had retired from practice in 1914, being acknowledged by all as a valued and distinguished Fellow of the Royal Institute of British Architects.

113 *An old 19th-century photograph, possibly of a wedding party, depicts the vestries added to St Giles church by Swinfen Harris.*

114 *The rear of Calverton Limes in London Road, now the Working Men's Club, possibly at the time it was owned by Colonel Hawkins. It was one of the major properties in the town where Swinfen Harris was commissioned to carry out alterations. The back of the building is now very different from this view.*

In his retirement, ever proud of his home town, he recalled its past in letters to the *Wolverton Express* newspaper and in talks to the new Literary and Debating Society which, after only one year's activity, in 1920 could boast 180 members. He recalled that there was not a single house in the town occupied by the same family, as had lived in it 80 years before, adding that 'old times have changed, old manners gone'.

He could recall the toll gates: one on the causeway of the bridge near Old Stratford, the other near Debbs Barn on the Wolverton Road. He made the point that whilst the removal of the toll gates gave better access, oddly enough there were factors which he thought favoured gates. For example, they had helped prevent the theft of horses and cattle at night time, and they had aided in the halting of runaways, whether human or animal. Tolls had imposed a tax on the direct users of the roads! During those 80 years Swinfen considered that comparatively few houses or house-fronts had been interfered with or rebuilt, though the lower stages of many had been altered for new businesses. In his view the skyline in 1840 as in 1920 'was intensely picturesque and varied'.

As County Surveyor, Harris had removed the old posts and railings along the causeway between the Ouse Bridge and the *Barley Mow* inn at the northern end of the town. This

115 *Swinfen Harris built a number of local schools following the passing of the 1870 Education Act. This example at Beachampton is now a private house.*

fencing had been a very necessary protection from the large droves of horned cattle on their way to the markets of London. Similarly, when the forests north of Shrob Lodge disappeared, the deer from the forest were deprived of their antlers and carted through the High Street *en route* to Windsor.

He remembered that the stone archway of the old St Paul's College had occupied the position of a red-brick house, formerly a grocer's, which had been as high as those houses that still remained; a wine merchant had lived at the stone-fronted house with his wine stores at the rear. The Post Office had been in the house north of the old *Coach and Horses* yard. Swinfen also noted such interesting features as the ancient gateway to the old *Cross Keys* inn, the mouldings on its oak lintel and its side posts. He admired the beautiful craftsmanship of the smith's work on the sign brackets for the *Cock* and *Bull* hotels.

He could recall many stories told him of the *Cock Hotel*. One was the visit of the 'great Duke of Wellington' to his old military friend, Lord Lynedoch at Cosgrove Priory, and Wellington's stop for a meal on his way back to London in a post-chaise. He also recalled the story of a similar visit to Lynedoch of his former antagonist, Marshal Soult; while breakfasting at the same hotel, he had been saluted by a merry peal of bells from St Giles' tower.

Eighteen

ADAM SHERWOOD, CHIMNEY-SWEEP

One of the 'characters' of 19th-century Stony Stratford was Adam Sherwood, who lived in London Road. Indeed the Rev. Loraine Smith of Passenham went as far as to provide him with a coat-of-arms on which was the motto, 'Hark away for a brush up'. This was a reference to Adam's great enthusiasm for fox-hunting. His hunting costume was said to be a chimney- pot hat, the height of which had been considerably lowered by repeated bangs upon the top and large wrinkles upon the sides; these were complemented by a green frock-coat and corduroy 'continuations'.

> To sweep the chimneys is my profession,
> With Brush and Shovel to raise alarms,
> I've gained the height by my discretion,
> So turn my Brush and Shovel to Arms!

116 *Adam Sherwood's coat-of-arms well represents the tools of his trade!*

HARK AWAY FOR A BRUSH UP

117   *Sherwood lived in one of these 'poor' thatched cottages close to Wolverton St Mary's church in London Road. Shown here in* c.1880, *they were demolished at the end of the century by their owner, the Radcliffe Trust.*

Adam managed to mix business with pleasure on the hunting-field, since he was always pleased to take an order to sweep chimneys, particularly of the large houses nearby. The largest at which he worked was Thornton Hall which had 101 chimneys. One day he had finished sweeping the chimneys at the Rev. Mr Drummond's. The latter said, 'You black-coated men earn white money very quickly, Adam'. 'Yes, sir,' he retorted, 'we gentlemen who wear black coats earn very quickly, don't we sir?'

Adam was a good whist-player and fond of the game; his dress on such occasions was a fine silk hat, carefully brushed and a nice cloth coat, sporting style. His waistcoat, worked by the Misses Loraine Smith of Passenham, was worsted with a scarlet ground, the thickest row of foxes' teeth down the front instead of buttons and 'nicely spotted all over with foxes' heads'. Sherwood was a popular person in both town and countryside. Despite losing £400 in a bank failure, he saved enough to retire and enjoy his retirement.

Nineteen

THE WORLEY FAMILY OF SOLICITORS

One of the remaining imposing Georgian houses in the High Street, a private house until the early part of the 20th century, is no. 25 which was the home of the Worleys, a family of solicitors, throughout the whole of the 19th century. Thomas Worley is shown as a solicitor and John Worley as a surgeon in the *Universal British Register* of 1793-8, added to which Edward Augustine Worley is noted as a solicitor in *Holden's Directory* of 1811. The latter is further described as a 'Gentleman' in the list of shareholders of the Stony Stratford Gas and Coke Company, founded in 1838.

However, the Thomas Worley whose pocket book came to light several years ago was of the next generation, born *c.*1800. The notebook showed Thomas to be a true countryman. He loved a day's shooting or fishing and was never averse to leaving someone else in charge of the office while he went out to watch the meet of the hounds. He walked regularly to the great houses nearby or got out his pony and trap to call on friends and acquaintances further afield, to take wine or to stay for tea.

In January 1839 he went to a shoot at Wolverton Great Ground, where the company included Lords Tavistock, Abercorn, Carrington, Russell, Fitzroy and Ipswich. He seemed to know all the right people: the Duke (of Grafton) at Pury, Lord Carrington at Gayhurst and Mr Knapp at Great Linford.

118 *John Worley (1829-1901), a solicitor, was very prominent in the town's institutions.*

119 *No.25 High Street had been the home of the Worley family for over a century. It is shown here in 1902 as a private dwelling before a shop front was inserted; today the doorway is still its recognisable feature.*

The railway had just arrived at Wolverton; on 23 March he wrote that he 'went to the Railroad – an accident. The engine thrown over the bridge into the canal.' This was the time of the first Wolverton railway station, a temporary wooden structure that was high on the embankment by the first railway bridge, as one leaves Old Wolverton today in an easterly direction, just before the entrance to the Wolverton Park sports ground. Thomas travelled to St Albans Races by train, and later to London at a cost of 16s. 6d. He also journeyed to Northampton, Birmingham, Norwich and Yarmouth, as well as to a horticultural show at the Vauxhall Gardens in London and to the races at Newport Pagnell.

Thomas paid 13s. 0d. for a bushel of flour; 2s. 6d. to have a broken window repaired; 4s. 6d. for 7lb. of beef; 6s. 0d. for four bushels of potatoes and a guinea for 11cwt. of carrots. A coach ride to London cost him another guinea. He paid 5s. 0d. for a pair of razors, 1s. 0d. for a knife and 2s. 0d. for a pair of scissors. He spent £3 5s. on a Victoria shawl for his wife and £1 6s. for a brooch, but he paid his servants only £9 a year or 2s. 0d. for casual labour. At Christmas he gave the church bell-ringers 1s. 0d. for their beer.

He liked good company: there were numerous entries in his pocket-book on items of expenditure, just noted, as in Stony Stratford, 'at the *White Horse*', 'at the *Cock*', and 'at the *Barley Mow*'; or in Newport Pagnell 'at the *Swan*'.

His son John, 1829-1901, was admitted as a solicitor at just over 21 years of age. He continued with his father in practice and eventually succeeded him; he also held the post of coroner for the Newport Pagnell Division of North Bucks for nearly 48 years, the area including Stony Stratford and district. His son was later his deputy. John was one of the oldest among the commissioners appointed under the charity for the paving and lighting of the streets of the town, as well as being the managing director of the gas company and also a trustee of various local charities. Only a few weeks before his death he had been appointed the trustee to wind up the accounts and other matters connected with the dissolution of the Stony Stratford Building Society. He helped found the Dispensary and Cottage Hospital, of which he was treasurer. Added to these activities he was also a churchwarden and sidesman at St Giles.

John Worley's elder son was Edward Thomas, 1855-1920, another member of the family practice. He had been educated at St Paul's College and was articled to his father. He went to Wellingborough for a few years, was admitted a solicitor in 1877 and returned to work with his father, succeeding him as coroner. He was clerk to the justices of the Stony Stratford Petty Sessional Division from 1887. Like his father he was active in many town charities, but he had his grandfather's sporting interests too, thus following the hunts and hounds in the locality. He was married with two daughters and lived at Ousebank, at the corner of the Market Square and Mill Lane.

The family home at 25 High Street was sold in 1902 on John's death. Noteworthy later owners were A.J. Negus and R.J. Fleming, whose ownership of this property progressed through the evolution of transport from the bicycle to motor vehicles. The grounds behind the property were eventually lost in the development of Cofferidge Close and so this house is no longer a family home.

120 *Details of the sale of John Worley's home on 7 July 1902, following his death. The auction was held at the* Cock Hotel.

Twenty

THE WALFORDS AND THE
NORTH BUCKS. ADVERTISER

One of the few illustrations of Stony Stratford High Street in the 19th century is a trade-card dated October 1862 which shows the name 'Walford' over the shop-front of what is now 73 High Street, today Haseldine's the bakers and confectioners. Alfred Walford had come from Banbury; in the 1847 *Kelly's Directory* he was described as a printer and stationer in High Street East, but by 1854 he had switched to the west side of the road. In a rival directory of 1852 he is described as 'printer, stationer, bookbinder, newsagent and agent for the Athenæum Life Assurance'.

121   *The long-closed* Swan with Two Necks *inn and the Stony Stratford Industrial and Provident Society shop flank Bridgeman's the stationer at 88 High Street, formerly the printing works of William Nixon, publisher of* The Cottage Newspaper, *in this postcard of* c.1910. *As can be seen, unusually at that time, one had to climb three steps to reach the shop door.*

122 *This representation of the 'middle' High Street was on a trade card issued by the printer, Alfred Walford (today no.73). Dated October 1862, it is one of very few early scenes of the town. Easily recognisable are the* Cock *and* Bull *inns. Opposite the* Cock, *the portico was on Oliver and York's Bank, which when rebuilt became Lloyds Bank and today is Lloyds TSB.*

William Nixon had published the *Cottage Newspaper* at his printing works on the opposite side of the High Street, from March 1854 until his death in 1868. The paper's subsidiary title was *Stony Stratford and Wolverton Station General Advertiser*; its final issue was 682 of 17 April 1868. Alfred Walford took the *Cottage Newspaper* over from Nixon's niece, renaming it the *North Bucks. Advertiser*; he published it as a broadsheet with a mix of national and local news. When Alfred died in March 1886, his wife Leah continued the business in its entirety until three months before her own death in January 1900, when she retired to The Colony, now 94 High Street. The firm was then bought by Mr

G. F. Eardley, and there was still evidence of the printing business years later, when it was purchased by Thomas Haseldine.

However, to return to the Walfords, Alfred was one of a family of newspaper publishers. George Walford and his family ran the *Banbury Advertiser* at 72 High Street, Banbury, for some 60 years from 1854. In addition, Arthur Walford and his father George, trading as Walford and Son, founded the *Buckingham Advertiser* in 1887; Arthur became its sole proprietor at the end of 1890 when his father retired. The *Buckingham Advertiser* and printing works were bought by E. N. Hillier in 1923.

Twenty-One

FROM THE PENNS TO
SHARP AND WOOLLARDS

The Penn family features in English and American history in the 17th century, whilst the Woollards became leading-players in Stony Stratford in the 19th and 20th centuries.

Stratford House, off the corner of the Market Square, was formerly called Ousebank Gardens or Ousebank. On the site of its garden there was once a tan-yard, and many of the walls around it were built of bullocks' horns: thus the lane leading to Stratford Mill became known as Horn Lane. The Penns had purchased the land in the town in 1600. John Penn was the tanner; he and his brother Francis Penn, a silk mercer, were buried in St

Giles' churchyard about 1630. The Penns diverted the river Ouse in order to establish a water-mill at the corner of their lane.

Samuel Sharp came from Towcester in 1819 to purchase the business. A young man from London, Frederick W. Woollard, joined him as a partner in 1845. By 1869 Samuel Sharp's descendant, William Sharp, was living at Ousebank and Frederick Woollard was nearby in Church Street. In 1920, both Mrs Alice Woollard and Edward Worley died; the Worleys by that time had moved to the Sharp's old home at Ousebank; indeed Mrs Worley was still living there in 1939. F.W.

123 *The rear of Stratford House in Mill Lane, c.1950; this was formerly called Ousebank. The house dates from the early 19th century; there is an arched porch to the garden with a cast-iron balustrade.*

124 *Frederick Woollard with his sons Charles (top right) and F. Ulph (bottom right) of the firm Sharp and Woollard. All were very prominent in running the town.*

125 *The archway by the Grafton Cycle shop led to the Retreat, a group of five cottages for the elderly administered by the trustees of the Retreat Charity, which had been built in 1892 by Frederick Woollard; the chemist J.W. Smith was a son-in-law. All these properties were built on the workhouse site. Next door is Hassall's china and glassware warehouse.*

126   *Sharp and Woollard's in Church Street, c.1981, eight years before it ceased trading here. The factory's core dates from its establishment in c.1730, but the high building, left, is from 1900, the new building near the gateway from 1980. The remains of the West side's workhouse are incorporated in the buildings, upper right. The Woollards lived at the higher house, no.36.*

Woollard outlived his wife by only one year; he died in 1921 at the grand age of 90 years. A grandson of Samuel Sharp, Mr C. Boden Britten, who was another partner in the firm and had lived in the town, since the beginning of the century, died aged 53 in March 1924.

In 1873 Sharp & Woollard, as the firm had become, won a prize medal for its harness leather at the first Northampton Leather Exhibition. The Exhibition was later transferred to London, to become the National Exhibition.

In 1984 an additional factory was opened at the nearby village of Cosgrove, trading as Samuel Sharp (Curriers) Ltd. The factory in Stony Stratford was closed in 1990 and all production centred at Cosgrove. In 1991 the company received an Enterprise Development Award for Exports from the Department of Trade and Industry. Its largest market was India, but other markets included Japan, Australia, New Zealand, the United States, together with Scandinavia and most European countries. The firm was sold in

1998 by its last owners, Peter and Norman Brazell, to the firm of Joseph Clayton of Chesterfield.

To return for a moment to the Woollard family, their achievements have been mentioned already in these pages, through the activities of Frederick and his son Charles. His two other sons, Ottiwell (d.1903 while at Midhurst) and F. Ulph, also made their marks on the town. Stanley, Charles' son, continued in the business; whilst Monty, the son of Ulph, became a gentleman farmer. The Woollard name represented a dedication to public service from County Council to Parish Council and in the membership of a host of local organisations. Frederick was the first person from the town to be appointed a County Magistrate; earlier appointments had been from the aristocracy or gentry, living outside the town.

The Woollards were Baptists and benefactors to the town. Frederick provided the land for the cemetery extension and in 1892 took down the old Workhouse buildings, which had provided housing for the poorer townsfolk after the new

workhouse for the Potterspury Union was opened at Yardley Gobion (in use 1837-1925). Frederick replaced these stone workhouse buildings in the High Street with the Retreat almshouses for the elderly. Incidentally it is interesting to note that the factory in Church Street had contained the remains of an early workhouse, the one for Stony Stratford West: this little group of buildings was first described by Dr Brown in *Stony Stratford: The Town on the Road.*

There was much friction at the turn of the 20th century between the Baptists and the church authorities, because the latter still administered a number of the town charities. Apropos this, there were strong protests by the nonconformists at the imposition of an education rate under the 1902 Education Act.

Frederick caused a stir at the meeting of the Stony Stratford East Parish Council in March 1897, by announcing that he was retiring from the Council, although he had served on it for only two years. He considered, 'so far as one can see, there is nothing for a Parish Council to do beyond hiring rooms, paying a clerk three or four pounds to call

127 *In 1873, at the first Northampton Leather Exhibition, Sharp and Woollard was awarded this prize medal for its harness leather.*

and attend meetings, running up a bill for printing, and finally spreading a little gravel over some footpath of doubtful ownership'. Indeed, he added, 'Every effort to bring about a cleaner highway with better sanitary arrangements has entirely failed'.

He saw the problem, as the procedure then in place for governing an area of 'a few hundred yards'. There was over-representation: 'You elect annually for Stony Stratford West nine councillors, for Stony Stratford East seven', he said, 'then, for Wolverton St Mary, three, Calverton St Mary, three, with four District councillors, making

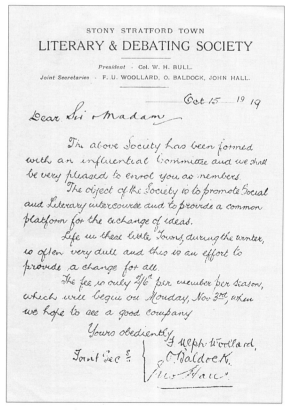

128 *Recruiting letter from the secretaries of the newly-formed Literary and Debating Society in the winter of 1919-20.*

a total of 26.' In addition, 'Independent of these councillors, we have our permanent staff of 12 Street Commissioners, who absolutely control all the paving and lighting of the town; thus making a grand total of 38 representative men to do but a handful of work.' There was more, 'I might add the water and gas committees, who … are ever doing permanent mischief to the highways.'

He saw the only remedy in an application for 'urban powers' when an elected Board of seven or nine members would be able to do the work better and more cheaply. There was a 'splendidly defined boundary on one side, viz. the Ouse from the Water Works, Calverton Road, to the *Barley Mow*, and around to Wolverton Mill, the greatest care being taken to give all properties assessed the utmost value for their money'. These phrases resonate, as they contain words which trip off the tongues of politicians even to this day!

Charles Woollard, 1856-1939, has been mentioned earlier in connection with the Ancell Trust. He had been educated at St Paul's College, and was in the family business of Sharp and Woollard for half a century. Late in the 19th century he lived in Cumberland Terrace, the name for the block of houses in the lower part of Mill Lane. He was noted as a Liberal, a life-long abstainer and a non-smoker. He was honorary clerk to the first Parish Council formed in the town. A life-long Baptist, he had joined the Stony Stratford Baptist church in 1875.

In the elections for the new Wolverton Urban District Council in April 1919, there were 32 candidates for 15 seats. Charles Woollard came fifth with 906 votes. A.W.

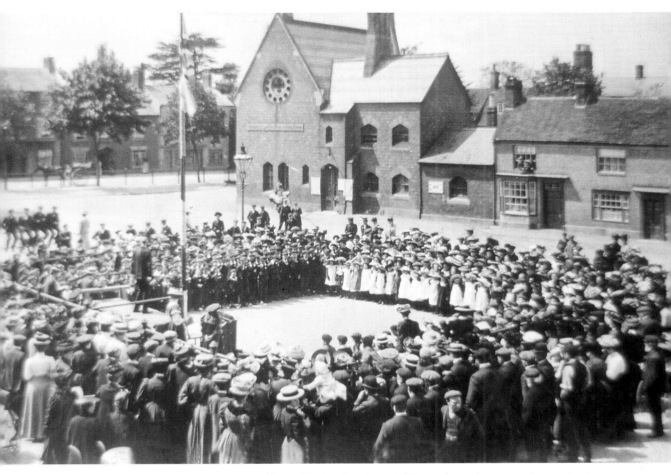

129 *A gathering on the Market Square to celebrate Empire Day in 1908. The magistrates' court can be seen in the background.*

Wilson, architect and surveyor at Wolverton Works, was first with 1,053 votes. The next three seats went to Stony Stratford residents: second with 1,025 was the Baptist minister, Rev. Stephen Cheshire; third and fourth were brothers, both businessmen, W.J. Elmes, a County Councillor with 1,023, and Arthur Elmes, late vice-chairman of the Rural District Council with 969 votes. After the ward system was established in May 1919 W.J. Elmes became chairman of the new council.

Whilst a report of C.P. Woollard's talk on the history of the town was published in 1920 it was a few years more before it appeared in book form, printed at the back of R. Ewart Barley's *Romance around Stony Stratford*. A comment was made in 1924 that Charles Woollard took no holidays, 'preferring to work day-by-day for the good of the town … and for the welfare of its inhabitants as a whole, irrespective of creed or politics'.

Twenty-Two

THE WOLVERTON AND
STONY STRATFORD TRAMWAY

The tramway still has a fascination for transport enthusiasts, though it closed down during the General Strike of 1926. Old transport postcards, rather than later photographic prints of them copied from the old glass plates, fetch high prices at postcard fairs. A section of tramway track was unearthed when the roundabout at the junction of Queen Eleanor Street and Wolverton Road was being built. This proved, of course, that the entire track could not have been lifted by the County Council in road-widening between 1927 and 1934, as had been thought. As this is being written, the rebuilding of one of the tram carriages is nearing completion at the Milton Keynes museum at Wolverton. At the same time the small depot at Old Stratford, used for the Deanshanger extension of the line (1888-9), has been demolished to make way for a small housing development. The main depot, at Stony Stratford was entered by the roadway in Wolverton Road, between nos. 21 and 23. Trams emerged from what is now St Mary's Avenue; the tram depot was used eventually as the United Counties bus company's garage; later still it has been Walter Franklin's builder's yard.

130 *An inspection of one of the Krauss tram engines by members of the Institution of Mechanical Engineers in May 1888. This is the only known photo of the 20-seater carriage which was used solely in the early years on the Deanshanger extension and was said later to have 'languished in the depot'.*

131 *A rare view of a tram at the northern end of High Street. The tramlines again are in the centre of the road.*

132 *One of the two Green of Leeds engines in Wolverton Road, c.1915. More powerful than the Krauss engines, they were the mainstay of the system for many years. The 100-seater carriages are beginning to show signs of their age, sagging noticeably in the middle. Tarpaulins shield passengers on the upper deck from the elements.*

133   *Trams, workmen, Odell's horse and wagon delivering to the villages: all present a lively scene, c.1907. The engine, centre, is no.4 of 1900, the only one from Brush of Loughborough; apparently not as reliable as Green's, it was kept as a spare. In the middle road is a Green with two carriages; beyond that another two cars, possibly pulled by the other Green loco.*

All of the line's six carriages were built by the Midland Railway-Carriage & Wagon Co. Ltd., Shrewsbury in 1887-8. Only one photograph appears to exist of the 20-seat single-decker and that is when it was under inspection by some official party: that vehicle, which had open sides and seating in the form of cross-benches, was said not to have been used after 1889. However, the other five carriages were double-deck vehicles – a 50-seater, an 80-seater, and three 100-seaters, which lasted until the end of the line. They had open-staircases without any glass in the sides of the upper-deck, although eventually tarpaulin sheets were fitted to combat the elements.

The 100-seaters were said to be the largest vehicles in the country, measuring 44ft. in length and 5ft. 9in. wide. With standing passengers they could carry up to 120 people at a time. The carriages were originally fitted with oil lamps and later with acetylene light, but they were installed with the oil gas system used on main-line railways, when the London & North-Western Railway took over the system.

In addition, there were some wagons and parcels vans, but only one very small photograph is known of a wagon: this appeared in the *Locomotive* magazine of 15 February 1924. Two wagons had adjustable flanges so that they could operate on rail or road. When the train reached the *Cock*, the wagons were hauled off the line by horses, enabling the load to be delivered by road. It must be stressed also that the tramway was a narrow-gauge railway system where the gauge was finalised at 3ft. 6in.; these carriages were hauled by steam-powered engines similar to those found in the industrial towns of the north and in the Black Country. Modern trams such as those in Blackpool, or on the modern metro systems of Leeds, Manchester, Sheffield and Birmingham, use electric power.

Over the line's existence motive power was provided by some seven different steam tram- engines although, unlike the carriages, all have been scrapped. Probably no more than four engines were in use at any one time. The two engines used at the opening of the tramway in 1887 between the *Barley Mow*, Stony Stratford and Wolverton railway station, were by Krauss of Munich. A third Krauss engine

134 *Varied transport scene, c.1920, in Wolverton Road near the* Forester's Arms. *Two open-top solid-tyred buses of the National Omnibus Co. are bound for Stantonbury or Bedford; behind them are a hackney carriage and tradesman's bicycle. The Bagnall engine of 1920 hauls one carriage; the passengers are led by the renowned conductor, Billy Newton, 'Little Billy'.*

135   *An official photograph in the Wolverton Road depot, c.1919, portrays carriage no.2 and emphasises the sheer size of these 100-seater carriages. The railway company modernised them as shown, in what proved to be the closing years of the line; by that time the only engines remaining were the Greens, Brush and new Bagnall.*

was bought for the short-lived extension, to the *Fox & Hounds* in Deanshanger, which was hoped to gain traffic from the Britannia Ironworks of E. & H. Roberts.

The first two Krauss engines were considered under-powered for their loads, particularly as they might have to draw up to three carriages at a time. So in 1887 two more powerful engines were bought from Thomas Green & Sons, Leeds and a third in 1900 from the Brush Electrical Engineering Co. Ltd of Loughborough. Following the acquisition of the line in 1919 by the railway company and the disposal of the third Krauss engine, the carriages were rebuilt in Wolverton Works; then a saddle-tank locomotive was purchased in 1922 from the Stafford firm of W.G. Bagnall & Co. Ltd. This distinctive locomotive remained in use until the closure of the line in the General Strike of 1926.

Initially it was hoped that the tramway would capitalise on potential customers such as those from local industry – E. & H. Roberts, Hayes, McCorquodale's printing firm at Wolverton, and the railway company for the carriage of their employees, for the public and for the haulage of freight. Yet the tramway had a shaky existence, over the years being run by six different companies, with consequent changes of name. The railway company took it over from the 'Wolverton and Stony Stratford and District New Tramway Company Limited', which since 1891 has been run by Sir Herbert Leon of Bletchley Park. Nevertheless for all its problems – derailments and breakdowns, or the inevitable competition from motor buses – the tramway is still remembered with nostalgia by those who rode on it. It even ran a bus service itself in 1916!

Twenty-Three

POSTSCRIPT

Between the two world wars the town expanded to the east in St Mary's Avenue and Frankston Avenue, and to the south on the Egmont Estate with Egmont, Claremont and Blenheim Avenues; further houses were to be built in that area in the sixties. The Wolverton Urban District Council was responsible for King George's Crescent linking King Street and Queen Street, and for Ancell Road, both in 1936-7 following the clearance of sub-standard housing in the town centre. After the war the Council proceeded to extend eastwards along Wolverton Road, building in Boundary Crescent, Debbs Close and Woodside from 1950.

136 *Nos. 3-22 Vicarage Walk at the turn of the 20th century, showing the railings which were removed during the Second World War for recycling in aid of the war effort. These houses were built in blocks of two or four; 11-12 were named The Roses, 13-14 The Ferns and 15-16 The Laurels the latter being erected in 1893. The roadway is still unadopted.*

137 *The* Fox and Hounds *inn at 87 High Street shows the building before substantial alterations were made. This may be a later name for the* Hare and Hounds, *first recorded* c.1770. *Next door lived Mrs Woodman, the aunt of Tony Rudd who worked for various motor-racing firms. Racing-drivers stayed here during the races at the Silverstone circuit.*

Private housing began in the 1960s in the shape of the Haven Estate that extended from Milford Avenue to the south-west; the Limes off Park Road and Egmont Avenue and Ousebank Way to the west behind Silver Street and Calverton House; this continued into the next decade.

Once the northern part of the 'loop road' had been built, now named Queen Eleanor Street, and Ostlers Lane was laid through the field by the Sports Ground, the intervening area was used for the building of Magdalen Close and for the Fairfield Estate off Wolverton Road. The trackways from Tower Passage or Vicarage Walk, across to Wolverton Mill and Old Wolverton, were severed by the new roads. Queen Eleanor Street effectively reduced the area of the recreation ground, which could be reached by pathways from Wolverton Road and from Vicarage Walk. To use modern parlance, the recreation ground is now viewed as one of the town's 'parks', hopefully spared from further development.

The other remaining fields include Walter Tombs field, reached from the old Gas Works site in the lower part of the High Street; it is now owned by the Milton Keynes Council and used as a football ground. Another open space is the original part of the Ancell Trust sports ground off Ostlers Lane, together with the field that was obtained from the developer of the Fegan's Homes site. Finally, there is the old St Giles Vicarage field, now in use as a playing field for the St Mary & St Giles School.

Off the southern part of Queen Eleanor Street the buildings on the Galley Hill and Fullers Slade estates were initiated by the Milton Keynes Development Corporation. These areas are now also part of the enlarged

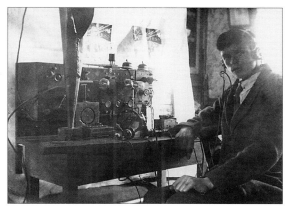

138 *All Dewick brothers, Percy, Leonard and Francis, were keen early radio enthusiasts. The first business of Len, pictured here, and Percy was at their home, then 9 Vicarage Road. Many will remember that the accumulators used to power radios were stored for charging in a shed there, before and after the Second World War. Len was to open a shop at 40 High Street.*

139 *Examples of the Renard Road Train appeared in 1903 and were eventually exported to countries such as Australia, Canada and India. This example, having carriages less enclosed than some models, is standing outside the Post Office in the High Street, c.1908. It has the registration DU85 from Coventry, because Daimler purchased the rights to the Road Train in 1908.*

140   *The junction of High Street, Wolverton and London Roads in 1951, showing some fine period vehicles. Left to right: Vauxhall Velox or Wyvern. Then, there are a lorry, motorcycle, an Austin 16 and a Triumph 1800. Albert and Daisy Read wait to cross Wolverton Road, opposite the* Plough *(that is the real article!) on their way to the London Road allotments.*

141   *Floods in the High Street were a common sight particularly in the winter months after a quick thaw of snow, as on this occasion in 1920. The* Rising Sun *pub is on the left, the entrance to Fegan's Homes on the right.*

142   *Posters for the 1910 Parliamentary election on the old* Rose and Crown *premises, 26-8 High Street. They support the Unionist candidate, the Hon. T.F. Fremantle, who lost to Liberal F.W. Verney by 5,944 to 6,055 votes, despite such accusations as 'What it has come to under so-called Free Trade', 'Verney voted against old-age pensions' or 'The foreigners got my job'.*

St Mary and St Giles ecclesiastical parish. Housing space is so limited in Stony Stratford today that houses tend to be built as the result of 'in-filling' or in those areas considered 'ripe for development'.

Furthermore, just as the railway development caused problems for the traders in Stony Stratford in the 19th century, so in the 20th century the traders faced similar difficulties, arising from the opening of the M1 motorway in 1959 and the new A5 diversion road from Old Stratford to Fenny Stratford. Added to these, the shopping centre at central Milton Keynes continues to be enlarged and there are peripheral shopping developments, such as the Tesco supermarket at Wolverton on the site of the original 1838 railway factory.

Stony Stratford once had an important role as a market town and shopping centre for the neighbouring villages in Buckinghamshire and Northamptonshire and had enjoyed the passing trade that increased with the volume of vehicles passing along the High Street and London Road between the great cities. They went east-west on the A422 along Wolverton Road to Old Stratford and beyond; or via Horsefair Green and Calverton Road to Winslow and Aylesbury. All means of transport regularly used these routes: car, van, heavy long-distance lorry and express motor coach.

*143   Because of modern develop-
ment, only the buildings on the
right-hand side of Wolverton Road
near the 'Top of the Town', shown
in this 1960s picture, remain today.
The cottages on the left, belonging
to the Radcliffe Trust, housed farm-
workers at Warren Farm Old
Wolverton. The man, left, is
Eastern National bus-driver
Harry Ford from Vicarage Walk.*

*144   A wedding in 1902: the lady by the door is Mary Mills; at the back extreme right are Robert and Amy Brown (née
Holland); at the extreme left are Mr and Mrs Jonas Mills; seated centre are Mabel and Robert Galtress, the bride Janet
Galtress and groom Alan Mills, Margaret Galtress and Elizabeth Mills; seated front, Elsie who married W. Foster, whilst
Harry and George, both killed in the War, are on either side of Lilian.*

145   *Ralph Perry's at 37 High Street, c.1910: a fine photo that shows the variety of goods available from this general ironmonger.*

146   *The smithy in Church Street where Rupert Roberts, the town's last blacksmith, is at work, c.1950. The forge was cleared for the small modern shopping development opposite St Mary and St Giles church.*

Now Stony Stratford has been by-passed: gone are the trunking runs by the huge commercial vehicles of Carter Paterson, Pickfords, Fisher Renwick, Hays Wharf Cartage and the nationalised British Road Services; as well as the wide loads that went through the town drawn by Scammell lorries of E.W. Rudd and Pickfords. The time has passed also when colourful lorries of the Marston Valley and London Brick Companies served the area, as it expanded after the Second World War. The town no longer sees the long-distance coaches of Midland Red on the London to Manchester via

Birmingham run; those of Standerwick and Scout journeying from London to Birmingham as far as Blackpool or Fleetwood, or from London to Birmingham destined for Morecambe and Keswick. There was also the country-wide Associated Motorways network, linking such places as Norwich in the east with the operational centre at Cheltenham and a host of seaside resorts beyond. Every day some passengers from Stony Stratford would board buses on the long joint route of Eastern National and City of Oxford Motor Services between Bedford and Oxford.

The effect on the district of the Wolverton Railway works factory fortnight, when the railway and McCorquodale printing works were closed and the employees went off on holiday, is a thing of the past. Gone too, is the seemingly endless procession of vehicles through the heart of the town to the Silverstone motor racing circuit, on Grand Prix days.

The town seems to have adjusted to these traumatic changes and to a lessening of its status over the years, for in these changes it joins many towns in the country which have been by-passed. It is fair to say that there is not the same range of basic goods available in Stony Stratford that there was 30 years ago: these are to be found now at central Milton Keynes or by making use of mail-order shopping. The bank and building society branches have decreased in number, but in their place are a number of estate agents and charity shops, as well as businesses dealing in those specialist fields that cater for the needs of modern lifestyles and modern technology. The branch of W.H. Smith containing a lending library was lost many years ago, but modern bookshops have taken its place. All the Co-op stores have closed, but there is now a branch of Boots the Chemists.

The inns, restaurants and public-houses are popular in the evenings and on Saturdays, and have a growing importance in the

147 *The manager and staff of the Stony Stratford Industrial and Provident Society Ltd., London Road, c.1912. A wide range of goods is on offer.*

148 *Wickins' sale, pre-1939, at 84 High Street, the drapery and no.82, the boots and shoes and outfitters shop, with Leslie Braggins in the doorway. The shops closed every lunch hour and some items were left outside: whole suits, pairs of shoes, but nothing was lost! Today only one shoe per pair could be left unattended. Wickins closed before the currency was decimalised.*

economy of the town. Judging also from the great number of vehicles that are parked, particularly in the evenings and at weekends on either side of the narrow streets, many of which were built without garages and before the advent of the motor car, the town is very much a dormitory suburb of Milton Keynes. Rising house prices also reflect the popularity of this corner of north Buckinghamshire, which Sir Frank Markham highlighted as the 'Jewel in the Crown' of Milton Keynes.

We end, as we began, with thoughts of transport, but this time of the future. Yet we can only bask in some kind of reflected glory, in mentioning that Air-Commodore Colin Foale once lived in Stony Stratford. He is the author of various works on space transport; but what of his son, Dr Michael Foale (b.1957)? For Michael was in the crew of the NASA space flight, STS-103, on a mission from 19-27 December 1999, which repaired and upgraded systems on the Hubble Space Telescope. STS-103 travelled 3.2 million miles in 191 hours 11 minutes! What would the compilers of the *Universal British Register* have made of that?

BIBLIOGRAPHY

Barley, R.Ewart, with Woollard, C. P., *Romance around Stony Stratford* (1928, reprinted 2003)

Bartlett, L., *Lace Villages* (1991)

Britnell, R.H., 'The Origins of Stony Stratford' in *Records of Bucks,* Vol. xx, pt. 3 (1977)

Brown, O.F., *Stony Stratford: The Town on the Road* (1987)

Brown, O.F. and Roberts, G.J., *Passenham, The History of a Forest Village* (1973)

Buckinghamshire Record Society: series of volumes published since 1937

Caine, W.S. (ed.), *Hugh Stowell Brown: Autobiography* (1887)

Elliott, J. and Pritchard, D.J. (eds.), *Henry Woodyer, Gentleman Architect* (2002)

Elliott, J.M.K., *Fifty Years' Foxhunting with the Grafton and other Packs of Hounds* (1900)

Guest, I., *Dr John Radcliffe and his Trust* (1991)

Hyde, F.E. and Markham, S.F., *A History of Stony Stratford* (1948, reprinted 2002)

Hyde, F.E., *Wolverton - A Social and Economic History* (1943)

Hyde, F.E., 'The Growth of a Town' in *The Town Planning Review* (July & October 1949)

Lipscomb, G., *The History and Antiquities of the County of Buckingham*, vol.iv (1847)

Lloyd, L.C. and Stenton, D.M. (eds.), *Sir Christopher Hatton's Book of Seals* (1950)

Markham, Sir Frank, *The History of Milton Keynes and District*, 2 vols. (1973/5)

Markham, S.F., *The Nineteen Hundreds in Stony Stratford and Wolverton* (1951, reprinted 1991)

Mynard, D.C. and Hunt, J., *Milton Keynes - A Pictorial History* (1994)

Newspapers: *The Cottage Newspaper, Northampton Mercury, North Bucks. Advertiser* and *Wolverton Express*

Pevsner, N. and Williamson, E., *Buildings of England, Buckinghamshire* (1994)

Ratcliff, O., *History and Antiquities of the Newport Pagnell Hundreds* (1900)

Rolt, L.T.C., *George and Robert Stephenson* (1960)

Rolt, L.T.C., *Thomas Telford* (1958)

Royal Commission on Historical Monuments, England, vol. 2, *North Bucks.* (1913)

Sharp, S., *Black Boots and Short Trousers* (Fegan's Homes) (1995)

Sheahan, J.J., *History and Topography of Buckinghamshire* (1862, reprinted 1971)

Tibbutt, H.G. (ed.), *The Letter Books 1644-45 of Sir Samuel Luke* (1963)

Victoria County History, *Buckinghamshire*, vol. 4 (1927)

Victoria County History, *Northamptonshire*, vol. 5, *Cleley Hundred* (2002)

West, B., *Remember Wolverton, Stratford and Bradwell* (1991)

Wolverton & District Archaeological Society: *Annual Newsletters*, 1956-69; *Wolverton Historical Journal*, Phillimore, 1970; *Milton Keynes Journal of Archaeology and History*, 1972-4 and 1980

Woodfield, P. & M.K.D.C., *A Guide to the Historic Buildings of Milton Keynes* (1986)

INDEX

Page numbers in **bold** refer to illustrations

B.M. 265·4
Black Horse Inn

W

P

256

Fur
Hou

Old Stratford

Sm

Draw
Bridge

B.M. 24

P

Old Stratford from the Ordnance Survey 2nd edition 1900.